C0-ARC-438

Portrait of the Past

A PHOTOGRAPHIC JOURNEY THROUGH WISCONSIN
1865-1920

Howard Mead, Jill Dean, and Susan Smith

Wisconsin Trails
Madison, Wisconsin

This reprint is dedicated to the people of Wisconsin in honor of the state's sesquicentennial. May we remember and cherish the past.

Copyright © 1971, 1998 Wisconsin Tales and Trails, Inc.
First edition, first printing 1971
Fourth printing 1998

All rights reserved. No part of this publication may be reproduced or transmitted in any form
or by any means, electronic or mechanical, including photocopying and recording,
or by any information storage or retrieval system, without permission in writing from the publisher.

Library of Congress Catalog Card Number: 72-185287
ISBN: 0-915024-61-6

Designer: William T. Pope
Printed in Canada.

Wisconsin Trails
P.O. Box 5650
Madison, WI 53705
(800) 236-8088
E-mail: info@wistrails.com

A traveling photographer carried his cumbersome equipment around the countryside in a specially designed wagon.

Contents

The Days of the Lumberjack . . . 6

A Rural Remembrance 22

A Village Visit 50

Men in Motion 76

City Sidewalks 104

A Life of Leisure 130

The Fabric of Life 152

Acknowledgments 176

The Days of the Lumberjack

EVEN IN DARKEST December and January, the lumberjack's day began any time from four o'clock in the morning on as the cook beat on a tin pan and bellowed "Daylight in the swamp; roll out your dead bodies." The timber beast ate off tin plates, drank out of tin cups, and used tin utensils. A crew of 100 loggers bolting their food in fifteen minutes or less must have made a tremendous racket. One bunkhouse poet called it a "rumbling symphony in tin." Eating, after all, was not a social event.

After a long day in the woods, the bunkhouse was another world. It was hazy with smoke, hot and stuffy near the big stove, cold and drafty away from it. And only a little of the fragrance of wet woolen clothing was wafted out through the skylight! The life of the lumberjack was not easy and it certainly was not romantic.

It was the lumberjack's job to cut trees. And cut trees he did. From daylight to dark, from first freeze to first thaw, the lumberjack worked in sub-zero cold and snow, snow, and more snow. Though thickly blanketed with white, the forest was not silent. The big pines, many of them 400 years old and up to ten feet in diameter, creaked and groaned, protesting each stroke of the ax and each cut of the saw. The cold air rang with the cry of "timber," the final thundering crack of the huge trees, and the curses of the teamsters urging their teams to pull mammoth loads of logs weighing seventy-five tons or more. Wisconsin's seemingly inexhaustible white-pine forest was leveled by these tough, lusty timber beasts in less than sixty winters, almost fifty in the last century and ten in this one.

One old lumberjack hit the nail on the head when he said, "We cut the top right off the state and fires done the rest."

The exploitation of the northern Wisconsin pinery and the fires that followed left a wasteland that staggers the imagination. John Curtis described it like this: "The desolation of much of the pine area is difficult to describe. In many places the entire landscape as far as the eye could see supported not a single tree more than a few inches in diameter. Only the gaunt stumps of the former pines, frequently with their root systems fully exposed as a result of the consumption of the topsoil by fire, remained to indicate that the area was once a forest rather than a perpetual barren."

These lumberjacks were spending the winter of 1886 at Wall and McNaire's logging shanty deep in northeastern Wisconsin's snowbound pinery.

An average day's work for a pair of sawyers was at least 100 pine logs—all like this one if they were lucky. This frosty team of horses is skidding a log on a "go-devil," a travoislike sled, at Ole Emerson's Camp near Cable in 1904.

The lumberjacks' day was broken only once, for the midday dinner, which was brought to them on sleds and eaten in the woods around a warming fire. This was the day's big meal. There might be red horse (corned beef), roast beef, or roast pork; murphies (potatoes); rutabagas; firecrackers (beanhole beans); dried apricot, peach, currant, raisin, or prune pie; cookies; swamp water (tea); cold sheets (doughnuts); coffeecake; raisin bread; and mountains of white bread and jam. This was Camp 3, somewhere in northern Wisconsin during the winter of 1904-05.

These loggers are sitting on the "deacon's seat" in a camp near Cable in 1895. Note their caulked boots and stagged trousers (cut off at boot-top level for easier working in snow). The bunks, called "muzzle loaders," were entered from the end.

Here, a crew of cookees is hard at work to satisfy the lumberjacks' prodigious appetites—peeling potatoes by the bushel, baking bread, and preparing gigantic ginger cookies nearly six inches across.

The cook was absolute king in the cook shanty, and he ruled with an iron hand. He allowed no talking at meals, and boasted that no man ever left one of his tables hungry. It is said that some of the lumberjacks learned to read from the advertisements plastered on the wall. This is the cook shanty at August Mason's camp near Brill in 1900, complete, it would seem, with strolling fiddlers.

In 1892, the crew of the Ann River Logging Company loaded these sixty-three white-pine logs, which contained 31,480 board feet of lumber. This huge load was 21 feet high by 20 feet wide, and weighed over 100 tons. They needed a winch to start it, but once it was in motion, two teams of horses actually pulled it for more than a mile on iced roads.

Every logjam—whether a small one or one like this monster that clogged the Chippewa River for fifteen miles in 1869—was dangerous. Once a jam started, it had to be broken quickly or the rising water would toss log after log into the tangle until the entire river would be choked off and the drive brought to a halt. Rapids would drop to a trickle and an ominous hush would pervade the river, broken only by the shouts of the daredevil "jam crackers."

From the moment they could tell water from land until darkness, the river drivers worked, almost always soaked to the skin. When a jam had to be broken or logs driven through a particularly treacherous stretch of stream, they toiled around the clock. For this, experienced hands received wages of about $2.50 per day and greenhorns, $1.75. This photograph was taken on the Wolf River in about 1902.

River Driving

On the day the spring thaw began in earnest, the mountains of logs that had been stacked all winter on the edges of the driving streams were tumbled into the rushing water. On this day, the strongest and most agile lumberjack laid down his ax and picked up a peavy for the spring drive. It was said that a really good driver could "throw a bar of yellow soap into the water and ride the bubbles to shore." Agile though he might have been, the river driver was almost always soaked to the skin, for there was no stopping to dry out; his wet clothes simply dried on his body.

Herding the vast flotillas downstream to the sawmills was the hardest, most hazardous task in the life of the lumberjack. The swollen rivers were massed with big logs, lurching, twisting, smashing together, riding the crest of the spring flood, and filling the air with a thunderous roar. Death waited for the unwary at every rapids, sluicing dam, and logjam. Yet the rugged, swaggering "river pig's" job was to keep the logs moving no matter what.

From the floating cook shanty, called the "wanigan," which followed close behind the drive, came four and sometimes five meals a day—breakfast at 4:30 a.m., first lunch around midmorning, second lunch midafternoon, and a substantial dinner at dark. The first and second lunches were usually packed in metal cans or haversacks called "nosebags" and carried to the men. This wanigan is shooting a wild rapids on the Flambeau River about 1900.

Resting casually on their peavies, a very neatly attired crew of the Moore and Galloway Company was photographed along the Wolf River in the 1890s. River drivers usually wore a battered, nondescript felt hat, stagged wool pants, and caulked driving shoes, sometimes with a hole cut in the toe to let the water out, and were generally pretty unkempt.

The thirty-foot-long bateau was the river driver's all-purpose boat. Built for heavy work and hard to tip over, the bateau was high prowed at both ends, had a three-ton capacity and shallow draft, and could get the men almost anywhere. This jam crew and their jam were photographed near Chippewa Falls in 1908.

When the river drivers hit town after the drive, they tried to make up for all they had endured. The saloons were a hubbub of boisterous songs and shouts and fights. And outside, the plank sidewalks were so thick with peavies that women had to walk in the streets. It was not unusual for a lumberjack to spend his entire $150 to $200 stake in a few wild days, enjoying the advantages of civilization. This photograph of a lumberjack's pet bear—also enjoying civilization—was taken about 1910.

17

A steam-driven portable sawmill belonging to the Moore and Galloway Company in Waupaca County, on the Wolf River, was very likely photographed by W. R. Parks of Iola in the early 1890s.

This photograph of a handsome little engine pulling a load of logs and carrying a bevy of berry pickers was taken about 1900 in northeastern Wisconsin. In the late 1870s, when good stands of pine close to driving streams became scarce, the railroads had begun to penetrate to the heart of the logging areas, providing reliable, all-season transportation. In fact, in this photograph, the glory days of white-pine logging already were past, for shown here is a hardwood operation.

This scene shows a group of raftsmen running Kilbourn Dam at Wisconsin Dells on a "rapids piece" or "string" made up of seven "cribs," which were the smallest units of a raft, placed end to end. Each crib, in turn, was made of sixteen-foot, rough-sawed boards stacked twenty-four layers high.

Beginning in the 1840s and continuing for more than thirty years, every March and April saw the Wisconsin River swarming with a continuous stream of rafts carrying rough-sawed lumber from the central Wisconsin sawmills to the booming markets on the Mississippi.

For quieter stretches of the river, rapids pieces were coupled together in threes to make "Wisconsin rafts." The raftsmen maneuvered these cumbersome rafts, which were about 50 feet wide by 125 feet long, with huge forty-foot-long oars, which served as rudders.

A Rural Remembrance

"AGRICULTURE MAY BE defined to be the art of cultivating the earth in such a manner as to cause it to produce, in plenty and perfection, those cereals, vegetables, and fruits which are useful to man, and to the animals which he has subjected to his dominion. Agriculture preceded manufactures and commerce, and rendered both possible; it is at the basis of all other arts, and was coeval with the dawn of civilization. Systematic husbandry seems to have immediately succeeded the savage state in all races; when population increased, and hunting and fishing became too precarious for a reliable subsistence, man supplied his needs by a tillage of the earth, and the permanent adoption of a pastoral life." Lyman Draper and William Croffut, *A Helping Hand for Town and Country: an American Home Book of Practical and Scientific Information*, 1870.

"The state of Wisconsin presents to the farmer a combination of advantages which are scarcely to be met within any other country. The occupier of a farm, whether large or small, is almost invariably the owner, and the land he cultivates he can, therefore, turn to what purpose he considers it the most fitted for. In Wisconsin there is not a single laborer on a farm who will receive less than from six shillings to a dollar per day; at the same time enjoying the advantages of excellent schools for the education of his children, gratuitously. The consequence is that the farm laborers and their families are well fed, well dressed, well educated in all the ordinary elements of knowledge, intelligent in conversation, and very superior to the same class in most parts of the old country." Samuel Freeman, *The Emigrant's Hand Book, and Guide to Wisconsin*, 1851.

In 1895, the Menominee River Boom Company employed so many men that it maintained its own garden near Marinette. In September of that year, the company gardener and his wife and child posed proudly behind a table laden with the fruits of their labors.

This crude but comfortable log cabin near Fence in Florence County was the home of Nels Wickstrom and his family. The Wickstroms wore their Sunday best for the photographer's visit in the autumn of 1891.

This pioneer family from Chippewa Crossing near Glidden, on a hunting trip in the early 1900s, indicates the isolation that faced northern Wisconsin's first settlers.

In heavily forested northern Wisconsin, genuine agriculture was not possible until the countryside was cleared. Yet, in the words of Samuel Freeman, "The bold, young American chooses a helpmate, collects some clothing, takes up his rifle and hatchet, and trusting entirely to his own prowess, commits himself and mate to penetrate into the heart of the western wilderness. There is something highly exciting and grateful to youthful daring and independence in travelling onward in search of a future home, and having found some sweet encouraging spot in the bosom of the wilderness, in rearing everything by his own handiwork."

Winter increased the isolation of these scattered northern homesteads—some women didn't see another woman for six months once the heavy snows came—but it was the best season for trapping. Nearly every homesteader maintained a trap line. The animal skins were pulled over wooden stretchers, scraped carefully with knives, and dried. Then they were taken into town or sent directly to Sears, Roebuck or to fur houses in St. Louis.

Beaver pelts were prime in February and March. The round, glossy furs on the side of this Ashland County cabin brought from $10 to $30 each in 1910.

The completion of a barn foundation was always welcome news, for the barn raising that followed was a major social event. Construction began on the first pleasant day in spring or early summer. Bringing their own tools, neighbors came from every side to help. In return, they received food, drink, entertainment, and the luxury of companionship.

The heavy bents, the main framed and braced sections, were carried to the edge of the floor. At a signal, about a dozen waiting men jabbed sixteen-foot pike poles into the top beam of the bent and slowly inched it upright. This barn is going up on Alva Paddock's farm near Kenosha in 1891.

At the end of each day, everyone sat down to a hearty feast. If there was a fiddler, the people danced on the new barn floor to tunes like "The Irish Washerwoman" and "The Wind that Shakes the Barley Field." This was George Vogel's barn raising in Door County in 1917.

As the bents went up, framed timbers were connected to the crosswise beams, horizontal and perpendicular braces were put in place, and each joint was neatly secured with drift pins. These farmers are working on a barn four miles northwest of Caroline in Shawano County.

Southwestern Wisconsin was the first region settled. Here, farming picked up as the lead boom fizzled out prior to the Civil War. Pioneer farmers chose land that contained some woods (for building material and fuel) and some prairie (for easy planting). The earliest farm homes were of unhewed logs, chinked with mud, roofed with shakes or hand-split shingles, and floored with rough planks. The furniture was scanty and crude—homemade benches and stools, boards laid across flour barrels and pork barrels for tables, platforms covered with straw or leaves for beds. Alex Smith's farm at Bear Creek near Lone Rock in about 1875 is typical of these pioneer farmsteads.

"The farmer in Wisconsin," wrote Samuel Freeman in 1851, "will find the prairies as fertile as the richest river bottoms. The labor of cultivation is but trifling. A heavy plough and a strong team are required the first year to turn over the soil. Corn is dropped into the furrow and covered over, and no other labor is bestowed upon it until it is fit to be gathered. The crop thus raised is not abundant, nor is the grain very good, but by the ensuing spring, the roots of the wild grass are found to be completely rotted, and the plough is put into a rich, light mould, fit for all the purposes of husbandry." This Wisconsin farmer and his wife are plowing and planting the prairie turf. Note their children peeking over the top of the grass.

"Standing in the midst of a rural landscape, with no crowding to compel slatternly habits, with plenty of room for flowers, hedges, garden, lawn, all upon a background of summer green, Nature conspires with the thrifty farmer to make his home supremely picturesque and inviting," wrote Lyman Draper and William Croffut in 1870. Though their homesteads differ widely in architectural sophistication, these three families show exactly the same pride in their farms and possessions.

Though photographed in 1890, this snug and sturdy cabin near Iola was built in 1860, probably with logs felled on the property. It was a monumental effort, for the neatly hewed logs weighed roughly 400 pounds apiece. The large glass windows are undoubtedly a recent addition.

Charles Tisch, too, wanted to include his spanking new carriage in this 1895 photograph of his barn at Teagersville in Marathon County. Many round and polygonal barns were built in Wisconsin. Farmers said the circular pattern gave them more room at the "working end" of the cows.

When the photographer came by in the early 1890s, this handsome young couple from the Black River Falls area made sure their prized horses and fancy carriage got in the picture.

Though women were in great demand on the frontier, childbearing, added to the other hardships of pioneer womanhood, caused many to die young or become old by forty. It was common for a settler to outlive one or two wives, and sometimes even a third. Yet eternally feminine, the humblest women used magnesia paste to keep their skin white, and blackened their eyelashes with elderberry juice or burnt cork.

Effie Howlett of Oshkosh photographed one of her neighbors making soap in 1904. Common soft soap was made by boiling fat and lye together in an iron kettle. The lye was obtained by soaking wood ashes in water, and you could tell when it was strong enough by dropping an egg into it. If the egg sank, the lye was too weak.

Though hard, the life of rural women was not without pleasures. Groups gathered frequently for quilting bees and spinning parties— happy, lively occasions when the women could exchange news and gossip, and show off their handwork. These ladies from the Lake Winnebago area are carding and spinning shortly after 1900.

Until the word "tractor" was coined in Madison in 1902, ponderous machines like this one shown threshing grain were called steam traction engines. These mammoth steamers consumed a ton of coal and up to 2,500 gallons of water a day.

"In butchering hogs, do not permit the hog to be run and worried by men, boys, and dogs before killing. This makes the meat tender and more apt to spoil. Scalding tubs should be placed under the strong branch of a tree or a derrick, to which a rope and tackle can be attached, and there should be at least two men to each hog. Let the scald be gradual, lifting out now and then to keep the hair from setting, and scraping off the hair actively." These directions for scalding a hog changed little between 1870, when they were written, and 1920, the date of this photograph.

Especially in northern Wisconsin, stumps had to be removed before farming could begin.
Already in 1870, commercial stump-pulling machines claimed: "A man and a boy, with
a horse, can take out from fifty to one hundred large stumps in a day." Considerable
improvements had been made by 1890, when this picture was taken. The site shown
is now within Iola's village limits.

"Goggled, scarved, and clad in linen dusters, seated at the right, farm fashion, early autoists started their journeys," wrote Fred Holmes. "Sometimes such a cloud of road dust was stirred up that passing cars had to stop or slow down until the atmosphere had cleared." These intrepid travelers of 1915 were visiting farm friends near Black River Falls.

Gypsy bands like this one camped near Shawano in August 1914 were far less welcome visitors in rural Wisconsin. Contrary to popular belief, they didn't carry off naughty children, but they did cut fences to camp in fields and sometimes plundered gardens, henhouses, and even kitchens, looking for food.

As wheat growing declined, other types of farming took its place. Potatoes were planted in northern and central Wisconsin. When prices were good, only the culls were hauled to this starch factory at Grantsburg, but when prices plummeted, whole crops were converted into starch. When this photo was made in September 1895, farmers were waiting as long as three days just to unload their potatoes at the factory.

Most farmers substituted the cow for the plow. Chester Hazen built Wisconsin's first cheese factory at Ladoga in Fond du Lac County in 1864, and, though it was initially ridiculed as "Hazen's Folly," there were fifty like it by 1870. Creameries like the one on the right were developed about a decade later. At first, Wisconsin's dairy products were not highly regarded. New Yorkers contemptuously referred to Wisconsin butter as "western grease," and the state's early cheeses were marketed under purposely misleading names like "New Hamburg" and "New York Factory." But thanks to refrigerated boxcars, the state's College of Agriculture, the Wisconsin Dairymen's Association, and such champions of scientific dairying as journalist William Dempster Hoard, Wisconsin was soon unrivaled as the nation's dairyland.

In 1880, Michael Baltus purchased an eighty-acre farm east of Auburndale Station in Wood County and built his family the plain but sturdy log cabin in the background. When this photograph was taken fifteen years later, the proud Baltuses—who had obviously prospered—were about to move into their fine new frame house with real glass windows and furniture imported from the East.

This Black River Falls woman is wearing widow's weeds. The style of her elegant dress, trimmed with lace and moire, places her in the early 1890s, but we have no idea why she chose to have her portrait taken beside this spiny plant.

Wisconsin's wheat boom began in the 1830s, and by the 1860s a Milwaukee newspaper could boast truthfully, "Wheat is king, and Wisconsin is the center of the empire!" The state was second nationally in wheat production, and Milwaukee rivaled Chicago as the greatest wheat-shipping port in the world. Wheat held absolute sway in Wisconsin until the 1880s. Then depleted soil and an invasion of chinch bugs ended its domain, and many farmers turned to dairying. Already in the 1850s, nearly every farm had a few cattle, but they were generally miserable scrub stock that foraged on whatever they could find. The cow's winter diet was the straw from the wheat crop, and the animals stood humped and shivering in the farmyard even in the coldest weather.

The frontier mill was a center of activity. Farmers came with their grain. Travelers stopped for food and lodging. Immigrants paused to have a horse shod or a wagon fixed. A visit to the mill was a festive event, including a picnic lunch beside the millpond. This group of men posed for photographer W.R. Parks on the steps of the striking mill at Iola in 1893.

Horses and cattle, probably of the French Black Celtic strain brought into Green Bay by French-Canadians, occupy the yards of this farm near Black River Falls, photographed by Charles Van Schaick in late autumn. The windmill, manufactured in Batavia, Wisconsin, carried an early form of advertising.

"The intelligent and experienced mother," reported a child-care guide in 1870, "chooses for the child with attention to the laws of nature. She gives him chiefly milk and fruits. She prefers the flesh of adult animals, which are rich in bone earth, to that of young animals, and accompanies it with garden vegetables. She gives the child bones to gnaw, and excludes from its diet veal, fish, and potatoes." But in spite of a mother's every effort, children faced a dangerous infancy and early childhood. In the 1880s, over 20 percent of the children died before they reached five years of age, mainly due to primitive housing and sanitation. In fact, the wonder was not that children survived precariously, but that they survived at all. Yet for children growing up on a farm, life was a continuing adventure.

The workers of the Ethold Granite quarry north of Big Falls in Waupaca County posed for a portrait in the 1890s. Note the crude derrick and the pile of paving blocks in the background.

Not all people who lived in the country were farmers. Quarrying and charcoal making were two of the industries that flourished in rural Wisconsin. Limestone quarries fed towering kilns that turned out lime. Sandstone built handsome homes, barns, and stores in southwestern Wisconsin. Granite quarries in places like Montello, Berlin, Redgranite, Wausau, and Devil's Lake produced headstones and monuments and blocks to pave the nation's streets. And stone quarried on the Apostle Islands constructed New York City's famous brownstone townhouses. In contrast to the pits quarrymen left behind, charcoal manufacturers of the late 1800s built large, beehive-shaped kilns of stone or brick throughout Wisconsin's hardwood regions.

Charcoal workers wheeled hardwood logs across tramways to load this set of kilns along the Fox River north of De Pere. At the base of the kilns, charcoal was removed and shipped by boat to a nearby iron furnace, where it was used to smelt iron ore. The kilns were active when this photo was taken in 1875, but by 1889, they were abandoned and falling into ruin.

It was a market day in 1902 when W. R. Parks made this photograph of the main street in Iola. Carriages, buckboards, and wagons line the dirt street, and farmers from the surrounding countryside fill the board sidewalks. The lumberyard was bustling, the clothier was doing a brisk business, and even T. W. Freeman, the dentist, probably had a few takers for his "painless extraction of teeth."

In countless crossroads communities, the lives of Wisconsin's farmers and villagers touched one another. It was to the towns that farmers brought their produce to sell or barter. It was in the towns that farmers bought the goods and services they needed. Horse-drawn wagons and one early truck competed with automobiles on the streets of Eau Claire in about 1920. The corn-laden vehicles were on their way to the city's canning factory.

A Village Visit

"THE FIRST SETTLER, like the first man to eat an oyster, was a man of courage, and a gambler too; he took a chance. He cast aside the precedents of the Old Country to make a new way of life. Liking his fellow man, he walked over the hill to visit the second settler and the two of them sang a song and traded labor at harvesttime. Then others came, and they found they needed a set of laws, a police force, and a court. They needed, too, a place to trade. They brought in a man of God to interpret the Word, and built a temple. They had hopes their children would go beyond what they were, so they banded together and built a school.

"These things grew into the crossroads village, with its church, its school, its blacksmith shop, and its trading post. The village became the big wheel that turned the smaller wheels of outlying farms. Like arteries feeding the limbs, roads threaded out from the village to the farms; over them their crops went to market, their children to school, and their families to church. And eventually telephone lines followed, and the free delivery of the daily mail." R. J. McGinnis

"Everywhere, the structure of the town was recognizable. The church bell pealed, summoning the congregation to prayer. The general store traded briskly in the luxuries and necessities of the day. The smith's bel-lows blew and sparks flew as wheel rims, hinges, and gun barrels were beaten into shape on the anvil. On their rounds through the village, people exchanged news and gossip. In the tavern, the lounger, the traveler, the countryman homeward-bound stopped for ale. You could always recognize a railroad town. It was laid out in a gridiron pattern. The north-south streets were given the names of trees, the cross streets were numbered. Some were built with a square at the center and stores on all four sides. In the square was a bandstand.

"By mid-century, towns had two rows of one-story wooden buildings. The occasional brick structure of two or three stories stood out ostentatiously. It provided offices for the lawyer or doctor, and the large hall on the second floor was an 'Opera House' or the lodge of a fraternal order. Along Main Street, the sidewalks meandered up and down steps. Wooden platforms, built to the height of a wagon bed to make unloading easy, ran from the sidewalk's edge to a store's front door. Some of the white clapboard homes were two stories high, made of smooth lumber from the sawmill. More pretentious houses were plastered or built of brick." Michael and Vera Kraus

A carriage was traveling along the dirt street and a woman was treading the board sidewalk when Charles Van Schaick photographed his hometown, Black River Falls, in the late 1890s. The Catholic church is shown on the right, and the steeple of the Baptist church, now St. John's, pokes up in the foreground. Van Schaick's own substantial home is in the center of the view.

This scene from Black River Falls shows the intimate relationship between small town and neighboring farmers. It also shows that although hogs had been improved considerably since the days of "prairie racers," roads had not.

Much of what hogs became can be seen in this 1902 view of Botz's Meat Market on the corner of South Main and Ninth Street in Oshkosh—from the bacon on the counter and the onion sausage and cans of lard hanging on the wall to the fresh pork sausage and early ad for Armour's "star" hams.

"Wisconsin hogs are descendants of the tall, lean, bristly, long-necked, and tusk-snouted 'prairie racers' brought up in droves from southern Illinois and Indiana between 1830 and 1860," wrote H. Russell Austin. "These hogs were so lean that housewives had to grease the skillet in which their pork was fried. But beginning in the 1850s, improved breeds—Suffolks, Cheshires, Berkshires, Essexes, Yorkshires, Chester Whites, Poland Chinas, and Jersey Reds—were imported. Hog raising proved so profitable that hogs were nicknamed 'mortgage lifters.'"

Fancy uniforms were the hallmark of the volunteer fire department. Firemen were lionized because they came dashing to the rescue whenever the alarm rang, and were equally ready to do the town proud in a parade. This group of fire-fighting dandies is the crew of the Old Brooklyn Fire House, which stood on Sixth Street in Oshkosh in the 1880s.

Smoke billows from the roof of this home in Black River Falls, as frantic volunteers struggle with the horse-drawn delivery truck that is pulling the hose cart to the blaze. The first team to arrive at the fire call after an alarm sounded was rewarded with $2.

A gaggle of wide-eyed boys surrounds this early "squirrel tail" pumper on the streets of Winneconne. It was with machines like this, in the words of Edward Baumann, "that volunteer firemen raced rival companies to the fire. Fistfights frequently broke out in the enthusiasm to 'lay first water' on a blaze, and sometimes a fire burned out of control while the rough-and-ready volunteers battled for position."

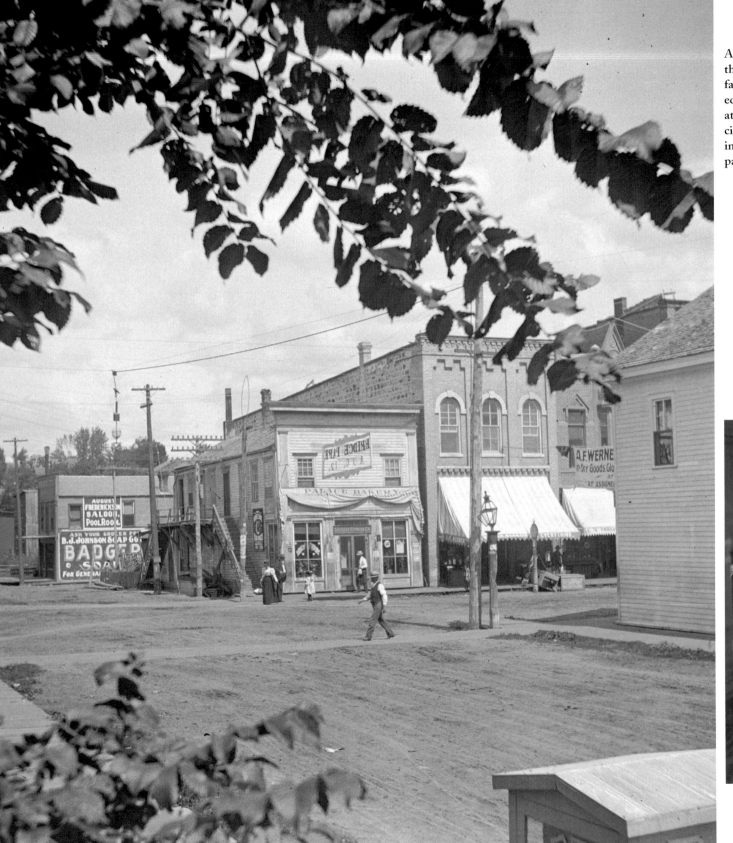

A weekly newspaper served to shape, not just reflect, the nature of a small town. Recognizing this, town fathers often gave free building sites to newspaper editors, persuasive types who could be counted on to attract settlers to the community. For their part, the citizens of places like Black River Falls, shown here in about 1893, knew that the weekly was the one paper anywhere that was truly interested in them.

Besides reporting genuine news, like fires and floods, weekly papers contained strongly worded political opinions, items about former residents, and all the local gossip that filled the air around the stove in the general store. But most newspapers, like the *Montfort Mail* of about 1910, had to bind books, sell magazines, and print handbills and posters and even Valentines to make ends meet.

The Wisconsin Press Association, first of its kind in the nation, had already been in existence for fifty years when this young man was photographed with an early linotype machine in Waupaca County around 1905. Machines like this put men like the *Door County Advocate*'s Henry Dankoler—who set a world's typesetting record in 1883 by hand setting 25,515 ems of type in just under nineteen hours—out of business.

In the presence of a photographer, most small-town people posed as they wanted to be remembered—starched and spotless and a little stiff. This informal portrait of John and Lizzie Diedrich, Grace Bowman (in black), and Howdy Doody look-alikes Philip, George, and Julius Nortmann is a refreshing exception. The Diedrichs were happy and relaxed when this picture was made in 1900, but during World War I, they were accused of pro-German sympathies, and were persecuted and ridiculed by their Black River Falls neighbors.

Beautifully beribboned, eight-year-old Anita, eldest of William Frederick Plamann and Anna Amelia Collin's four daughters, struck a martial pose with her pet rabbit in about 1915.

Miss Lily Kruschke was the epitome of elegance when she had her portrait taken in 1907. From the richness of her dress, it may have been an engagement picture, for she married and settled in Sheboygan a short time later.

Sarah Sophia Parker, the tenth and last child of James Harvey Rawson Parker and Sarah Sophia Spees, was fourteen when she was photographed in Wautoma in 1891. Less than a year later, she died of "quick consumption."

Two street scenes from quiet Kilbourn, now bustling Wisconsin Dells, reflect the leisurely pace of village life. Here, the sidewalk-laying crew paused from their efforts to pose for local photographer Henry Hamilton Bennett.

Vern Loomis and J. E. Jones stopped for a chat and a cup of water from Kilbourn's unique Memorial Fountain. Dogs drank from the basins at the foot of the fountain; horses, from the two large protuberances; people, from the small receptacles beneath the fish's mouths; and birds, from the bowl in the statue's hand. Today the fountain can be found in the courtyard behind the public library at 620 Elm St.

Shopkeepers and tradesmen—
like this Lake Winnebago-area
cobbler at work shortly after the
turn of the century—flourished
in small-town Wisconsin.

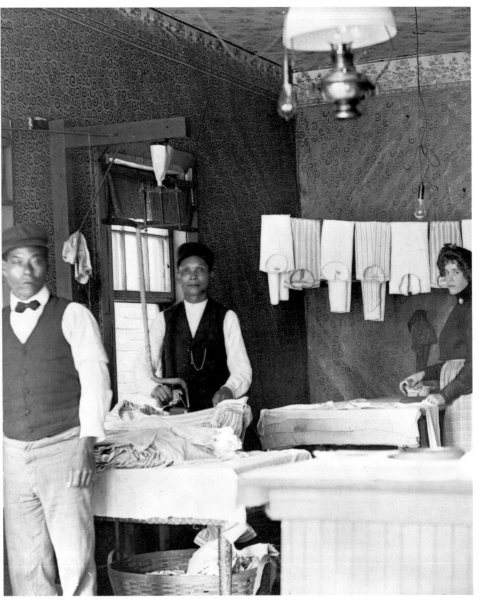

Business brought surprising diversity, even to the
tiniest villages. This was Yep Sing's Chinese Laundry
in turn-of-the-century Black River Falls. A friend
(left) was visiting at the time this photograph was
made, but Yep and his attractive employee kept right
on ironing. When Yep died, the whole town chipped
in for his funeral.

"The store of early days was more
than a market; it was a social
institution," wrote Fred Holmes.
"Back of the counter were large
barrels of sugar and crackers, and
boxes of prunes, dried peaches,
apricots, and apples. Toward the
rear was a hogshead of molasses
or sorghum; so many turns of a
crank measured out a gallon.
Nearby were several open boxes
containing different brands of
plug tobacco. Tinfoil-wrapped
packages of Plowboy smoking
tobacco lay next to boxes of
saleratus (baking soda), cans
of salmon, and bottles of vanilla
extract. From the ceiling hung
milk pails and lanterns. In the
corner stood axes and ax handles,
shovels and spades. Toward the
front were shelved packages of
Arbuckle and McLaughlin
(XXXX) coffee. In a showcase
were stick licorice, horehound
candy, peppermint discs, and
spruce and blackjack gum. In
the basement were barrels of
salt pork, dill pickles, vinegar
and kerosene, and a stack of
lutefisk piled like cordwood."
This particular social institution
was Earnst's Grocery Store,
which stood at the corner of
Main and Waugoo in
Oshkosh around 1908.

Womanhood aroused has ever been a formidable force, and the Women's Relief Corps, parading down the main street of Black River Falls behind a stuffed eagle masquerading as Old Abe, was no exception. Old Abe was a formidable force himself. At the Centennial Exposition of 1876 in Philadelphia, more people came to see Wisconsin's war eagle than to witness a demonstration of a new invention called the telephone. His moulted feathers sold for $5 apiece, and his presence, even via a stand-in, turned any parade into a patriotic extravaganza.

But much more characteristic than militancy in the early 1900s was this kind of feminine gathering. Charles Van Schaick photographed his wife, Ida (standing), entertaining the members of the DMC club in her wind-protected back yard. Nettie Lake had named the group after a brand of French crochet cotton used in fancy patterns, and though the ladies insisted the letters stood for "Damn Mean Crowd," no one watching them daintily sipping tea and lemonade and nibbling cookies would believe it.

The old-time saloon was the poor man's club. Men gathered in the barbershop or sat around the general-store stove for serious political discussions, but for good fellowship and friendliness, they went to the saloon. Men from all walks of life, as well as boys and even dogs, were welcome at its door.

Small-town mothers frightened mischievous children into good behavior by the mere mention of the constable's name, but, in fact, early officers of the law were usually tolerant—especially of the conviviality and high spirits that reigned in the neighborhood saloons. Oshkosh's finest, led by the clear-eyed stalwart on the right, lined up in their natty blue uniforms, complete with nickel-plated stars and jaunty hats, for a formal portrait in 1885.

"Women who could afford it patronized the town's dressmakers and milliners instead of sewing for themselves. They wanted imported materials for their clothes, and pretty buttons instead of hooks. And they wanted fine straw for their hats instead of rye straw. No calico sunbonnets, either. They carried parasols to protect their peaches-and-cream complexions." Michael and Vera Kraus might have been talking about these high-spirited young ladies from Black River Falls. Forward-looking women, they had dispensed with whalebone corsets, a fact that would've saddened Freeman Tripp (owner of a women's apparel shop in Eau Claire and holder of numerous corset patents) but cheered Amos Wilder (editor of the *Wisconsin State Journal* and father of Thornton Wilder), who wrote in 1899: "Where well-informed club and college-trained women set the fashions, the wasplike waist has gone glimmering. But in the rural districts, misinformed young women still cramp themselves into an abnormal, unhealthy, and revolting parody of the human form divine, unmindful of the official measurements of the faultless Venus de Milo (26 inches, if memory serves us right)."

The employees of the Rhyner Dress Making Shop in Oshkosh—shown here in July 1893—were a particularly stylish lot. The leg-o'-mutton sleeve had just been introduced earlier in the year, and already nearly all the ladies were wearing the new fashion.

Wherever there were a few women, there was a market for the latest clothing styles. This rustic millinery shop stocked ribbons, nosegays, bonnets, shawls, and hats piled high with flowers and bows—just the thing for the fashion-conscious woman of 1893.

"Peddlers drove about the country, making regular calls," wrote R. J. McGinnis. "Those who represented the larger patent medicine houses generally had a bright red or yellow buggy and a spanking team of horses. They were personable characters with what was known as 'the gift of gab,' and they could smell a chicken dinner for miles." Such a man was L. W. Smith of Oshkosh, shown here at the corner of Vine and Park Lawn in Iola, making his rounds in about 1900. Smith was usually paid with silver dollars, and sometimes collected as many as 600 a day.

In early Wisconsin, medical practice was unrestricted. Any blacksmith who wearied of his forge, any farmer who tired of his plow, might feel the gift steal over him and become a healer. There were botanic, herbalist, and hygeo-therapeutic healers; electric, eclectic, and electropathic healers; faith healers and spiritual healers; even old Thomsonian healers. And if a man did not become a healer, he could become a "medicine man," a salesman of patent remedies, like the man driving this wagon full of gorgeously coiffured young girls for the None Such Brothers Show, which toured Janesville in 1902.

Home remedies were used liberally, for doctors were sometimes days away from isolated areas. Prepared from herbs and roots, these cures showed the strong influence of Indian medicine. The bitterness of a potion was thought to be proof of its healing potency, so it was no wonder the sellers of patent medicines—like Sioux Indian Charlie's traveling road show, which visited Iola in 1890—found a ready market for their sweet syrups and cure-alls, many of which contained a shockingly high alcoholic content.

Close to the countryside, small-town people enjoyed pastoral pleasures. These ladies, young and old, carefully gathered up their skirts while wading in the cold, clear water of Baird's Creek around 1895.

The Crandall and Bennett families of Wisconsin Dells spent an idyllic afternoon together gathering trailing arbutus, one of the earliest wildflowers of the season, in the spring of 1899.

Towns grew up naturally along rivers, for a waterway provided transportation and power to run the mill. But a river provided other things as well—things like the special charm of an ever-changing, ever-interesting view, things like a great place to go swimming on a lazy summer day. The village of Alma forms a backdrop for these boys about to take a plunge in the Mississippi.

In many river towns, a covered bridge was a social center. Travelers and farmers waited out rainstorms under its solid roof. Every salesman that passed found room to add another poster to its walls. Country swains carved their initials on its timbers and stole kisses in its shadowy seclusion. The sign on this handsome bridge across the Wisconsin River at Boscobel witnesses to an era before automobiles.

Men in Motion

DURING THE FIFTY YEARS between the Civil War and World War I, America, and Wisconsin with it, experienced a period of fantastic material growth that has justly been named the Gilded Age. And nowhere was progress more apparent than in the field of transportation. Steamships, railroads, automobiles, and finally the airplane enabled man to move faster and farther than he ever had before. The world shrank overnight.

But this new-found freedom of motion was not won without growing pains and conflicts between the old and the new. People often reacted to the inventions with derision and doubt, rather than delight. One man grimly advised building more insane asylums to contain the people who would be driven mad with terror at the sight of locomotives rushing madly through the country with nothing to draw them, and a New London farmer sent this indignant letter to the traffic manager of the Green Bay and Western Railroad:

"Dear Sir,

I got 22 cows what I chase every morning and every night over your railroad tracks. Up until 2 weeks ago everything is fine, no trains is coming at 8 a.m. when we drive our cows over the crossing.

Then last Thursday comes a little pip squeak of a train with maybe 6 empty box cars going like a bat out of hell. He comes at just 8 a.m.

This I think is maybe a special so I hold my cows from cross-ing. Now day before yesterday comes the same dam train with those 6 empty box cars and I just get my 22 cows over the tracks when he comes barreling through.

What I want to know is who is this guy, the railroad presidents son, so they give him his own little train to play with, or some stupid conductor what forgets to take these box cars along on the regular run. ...

I would appreciate very much if you would tell this hot shot engineer to kindly take another cup coffee in the morning so he should get here later than 8 a.m. and not maybe make hamburger out of my holsteins. ..."

The automobile also came in for its share of criticism. Clergymen denounced the car craze as "deleterious to morals and religion," and doctors warned that the terrifying speeds attained by autos would cause insanity. In 1901, a brain specialist writing in *Automobile Magazine* predicted that "When these racing motor cars reach a speed of 80 miles per hour, they must drive themselves ... for the human animal is not designed to travel 80 miles an hour. ..."

But mass production and the desire for mobility and efficiency won in the end. Long before World War I, railroad tracks and early highways crisscrossed the land, and Wisconsin looked to the newest transportation frontier—aviation.

A carriage moved sedately down a curving country road near Wausau just before 1900.

Horsecars and carriages converged on Union Depot in Milwaukee to meet the other principal mode of transportation in 1890, the railroad. On the urban scene, horses were downright indispensable. Rain or shine, they pulled everything from big, rumbling brewery wagons to ice wagons and water wagons to the itinerant peddler's cart. The most envied man in town owned a luxurious rig and a perfectly matched pair of blacks or bays.

How different the sights and sounds and smells must have been when horsemen cantered down shaded State Street in Madison in 1892. Families went to church in surreys and phaetons, and whenever a group of farmers gathered to chat, they were almost sure to boast chestily that they owned a "Clark" (Oshkosh) or a "Stratman" (Dodgeville) carriage; a "Mitchell-Lewis" (Racine) or a "mandt" (Stoughton) wagon; a "Streich" (Oshkosh) or an "Anti-tip" (Stoughton) bobsled.

The early winter stillness of Black River Falls was broken only by the clopping of hooves and the muffled creaks of a buckboard. During horse-and-buggy days, as the snow piled up, it was simply packed down, not plowed.

Though bicycles in one form or another had been around since 1816, bicycling became the national pastime in the Gay Nineties. Young and old cycled, often carrying squirt guns full of ammonia to repel aggressive dogs. Men dressed in knickers, knee socks, and small, round caps with visors. Gibson girls danced to the "Velocipede Waltz" when they weren't out cycling, and wore Mrs. Amelia Bloomer's shocking new clothing fashion—voluminous trousers that were cuffed just below the knee, daringly revealing a shapely leg—when they were. Professional men, their pants clipped in guards to prevent entanglements with the wheels, pedaled to work, and factories and offices set up long rows of bicycle racks for their employees.

By the end of the 1890s, there were 312 bicycle manufacturers in America. The Meiselbach Bicycle Shop in Milwaukee was one that flourished with the fad. It was not unusual to find boys as young as these on the factory force, for children regularly were sent to work as early as nine or ten years of age.

"Henry the Cycle Man" operated his successful Schrottky Bicycle Shop at several different locations in Oshkosh. This photograph was taken at his Church Street store about 1915. Excited citizens gathered at the bicycle shops each year on Washington's Birthday, the official opening of the cycling season and the day the shiny new models were unveiled.

People planned their leisure time and social life around the bicycle. Even the smallest town had its cycle club, and nationally, the League of American Wheelmen published a bicycling magazine and lobbied for better roads. Ironically, when a Milwaukee cycle club held its annual race to Thiensville in 1915, the group posed before a billboard that foreshadowed the shape of things to come. One die-hard member had brought along his fancy high-wheeler, probably built about 1890.

In 1901, William Harley and brothers Arthur, Walter, and William Davidson began working on their first motorcycle in a small shed in their back yard on the outskirts of Milwaukee. They didn't have a machine for sale until 1903, but by the time this model appeared in 1905, Harley-Davidson was turning out upwards of ten motorcycles a year. The bikes were nicknamed Silent Gray Fellows because the company painted them all gray and tried to keep them quiet and inoffensive.

Clarence E. Garton, whose father had founded the Garton Toy Company in Sheboygan in 1879, posed with his high-wheeler just before 1900. Garton and other bicycle manufacturers were selling a million bikes a year in the 1890s in spite of the stiff price—$100 to $150 in a day when a good suit cost $15.

Milwaukee was a center for wheat trading in 1865, and most of the year the harbor was a bustling place. Smoking steamers and sailing ships brought immigrants with their baggage, plows, wagons, and household goods, as well as manufactured goods from the East, and left with their holds filled with grain. But in this photograph, winter has come to the Milwaukee harbor (note the men standing on the ice), stranding a pair of steamers.

The *Moonlight*, largest schooner ever built in Milwaukee, was constructed at the Wolf and Davidson shipyard in 1874. This photograph shows her a year later, when she sailed under Captain Sullivan. Unfortunately, this graceful ship met an ignominious end. In 1888, she was reduced to a tow barge, and in 1903, foundered in the Apostle Islands while carrying a load of iron ore. In the 1880s, just before the heyday of the steamer, there were about 2,000 wind-driven vessels—brigs, sloops, barks, and schooners—sailing on the Great Lakes.

A tug towed the steel-hulled whaleback steamer *Christopher Columbus* into Milwaukee in July 1904. The only passenger-carrying whaleback ever, the *Columbus* was built originally to carry 5,000 World's Fair visitors from Chicago to Jackson Park, a distance of some seven miles, in half an hour. And what a beauty she was—spacious refreshment rooms amidships, four gangways, a four-foot-wide promenade deck running all the way around the saloon, and an elaborate fountain in the center of the grand cabin.

The steamship *William H. Wolf* was launched at the Wolf and Davidson shipyard in Milwaukee on August 6, 1887. Had the photographer waited five seconds longer before taking his photograph, he could have captured the collapse of the coal sheds on the far side of the river. The wave created by the launching struck the scaffolding of the Northwestern Fuel Company's dock with terrible force, smashing the dock and throwing spectators into the river. Two people died, and many more were injured.

A McDougall whaleback is shown under construction in September 1892 in the shipyard of the American Steel Barge Company in West Superior. Inventor Alexander McDougall, an experienced Great Lakes pilot, had never seen a whale, but he called his cigar-shaped, blunt-nosed freighters whalebacks. Lake men called them pigs. The ponderous vessels easily navigated rough lake waters, but were hard to handle at the docks and difficult to load and unload through their narrow hatches, so no new ones were built after 1898.

With Wisconsin's wealth of water borders, steamboats played an important and colorful part in the state's growth. Operating on numerous inland waterways between 1850 and 1900, they carried everything from coal and cattle to lumberjacks and picnickers. The *Evelyn*, a river steamboat, passed through a set of locks on the Fox River. She made the Green Bay to Oshkosh run from 1883 to 1907, complete with a set of antlers fastened to her pilot house.

Fox River steamers weren't the plush, majestic vessels of the lower Mississippi—one was described as "a cross between a mud scow and a pile driver"—but they were sturdy craft, built to withstand the choppy surface of Lake Winnebago. The *John Lynch* was photographed as she left the docks at Butte des Morts one calm day in 1890, headed for Tustin, on Lake Poygan.

Most Wisconsin steamers carried freight on weekdays, then cleared the decks and spruced up for the weekend excursion trade. A Berlin paper reported on one of these outings in 1880: "One-half the passengers were drunk, three-quarters feeling good, nine-tenths brimming over with fun and frolic, and the whole so jam full of jollification and lager beer that they didn't know which way they were looking." On this considerably more genteel excursion in 1901, ladies with parasols and gentlemen in straw hats crowded the *K. M. Hutchinson* near the Main Street bridge in Oshkosh.

It was impossible to live during the age of steam and not be affected by it. The railroad provided access to markets and quick transportation, and it ended the isolation of many small towns. Where it went, towns grew and prospered. Where it did not go, great dreams died. The first locomotive of the Pine River Valley and Stevens Point Railroad was transported from Lone Rock to Richland Center by this ox-drawn wagon in 1876. The photograph was taken en route at Sextonville.

Railroads even changed time. Fred Holmes noted that "Until the 1880s all time throughout the country was local time; when a clock in Madison said 11:10, it was 11:16 in Milwaukee and 11:17 in Chicago." On Sunday, November 18, 1883, railroads throughout the United States adopted "Standard Time." Thereafter, people went to the railroad station to get the right time when the signal came over the telegraph wire. This first train of the Green Bay and Western arrived at Iola's sparkling new station on time in 1896 thanks to the railroads and not the government, which didn't officially recognize standard time zones until 1918.

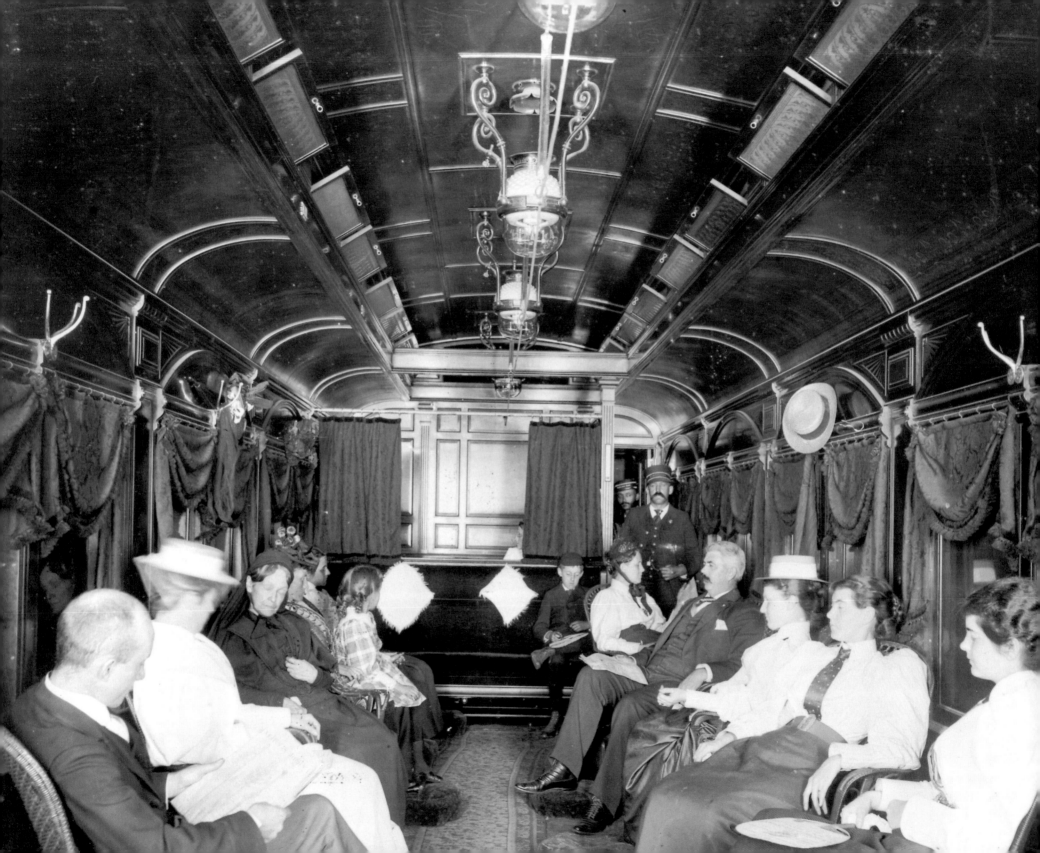

A parlor car of the 1890s provided elegance and comfort—richly burnished wood paneling, plush footstools, rattan chairs, and even heat, provided by hot water piped from the locomotive's boilers. The outfits and hairdos of the young ladies on the right emulate to perfection the classic style of the Gibson girl.

Along the Mississippi, the railroad tracks snaked below scenic bluffs—just the sort of view to photograph to show prospective customers the wonders of railroad travel. This private train carrying Henry Hamilton Bennett of Wisconsin Dells on the railroad-sponsored, picture-taking trip stopped at the tiny Buena Vista station in 1889.

Wisconsin winters often buried railroad tracks beneath huge snowdrifts. Smoking, puffing mightily, and with a cadre of shovelers standing by just in case, some trains took a long run and were able to plow through. Others found themselves buried to their smokestacks, and had to be extricated by the shoveling crews.

Inadequate brakes and signal systems made early railroad travel hazardous. This head-on crash on the Omaha Railroad tracks occurred at Teegarten's farm near Menomonie on September 9, 1881.

Wisconsin's impressive record of automotive innovations began in 1873, when J. W. Carhart drove the first, light, self-propelled car in America, and probably in the world, out of his garage in Racine. Horses bolted, children cried, and women screamed, but the Wisconsin legislature was impressed enough to offer $10,000 to a car that could survive 200 miles on the public roads. The legislators stipulated that it must be "a cheap and practical substitute for the use of horses on the highway and farm." The result was the world's first auto race, run between Green Bay and Madison in July 1878. The contest pitted two steam-powered vehicles that looked more like threshing machines than automobiles. When the racers reached Oshkosh, a newspaper reported, "as the average citizen of Oshkosh will get out of a dentist's chair to see anything fast, there was a goodly crowd at the race course." The Oshkosh-built entry, shown here en route, finished the race in a mere thirty-three hours and twenty-seven minutes. However, the legislature decided that the vehicle wasn't exactly inexpensive at $1,000, and—setting an example of cheapness—cut the purse to $5,000.

Mustached William Besserdich and derby-hatted Otto Zachow sat at the wheel of their four-wheel-drive steamer at Clintonville in 1908. The pair had developed the first four-wheel-drive vehicle in the world. When midwinter tests of this prototype were successful, the men built a dandy deep-maroon, seven-passenger car with a four-cylinder gasoline engine—the first FWD. Shortly afterward, however, the firm abandoned automobile manufacture to concentrate on producing trucks.

In 1910, the shipping room of the Kissel Motor Car Company in Hartford was crowded with the sleek, sporty models designed by William Kissel and his brothers. Kissel's most famous product, called the Gold Bug, was an elegant streamlined auto that cost more than $3,000 and rivaled the Stutz Bearcat and Mercer for beauty and excitement.

The Rambler, Wisconsin's first mass-produced car, was offered to the public in March 1902. This photograph shows Thomas Jeffery's Kenosha assembly line. Many early auto manufacturers, including Jeffery, were formerly in the bicycle business, which may explain why many early autos used bicycle tires and most early auto plants resembled bicycle shops.

The 1902 Rambler sold for $750, complete without front fenders, windshield, and top. It featured a one-cylinder, twelve-horsepower engine mounted in the rear, and was steered by a tiller (many owners quickly replaced the tiller with a steering wheel). For color, the buyer had Hobson's choice—Brewster green.

Until the 1920s, the motorist's worst enemy was the road. A motoring trip was a rugged adventure, and no car was complete without a tool kit and the inevitable spare tire. And before the advent of a highway-numbering system in 1917—a Wisconsin innovation that seems so logical it's taken entirely for granted today—a motorist had to know where he was going before he could get there. But despite the obstacles, the family automobile was a prized possession, as this photograph of the William Smith family out for a spin along the Ripon Road in 1908 makes clear. The custom of leisurely Sunday drives became so widespread by 1918 that the government had to curtail the practice for the duration of World War I in order to conserve gasoline.

Running boards were all-purpose devices. Some people served up roadside picnics from them. Others strapped luggage to them. And proud owners sat on them to be photographed, as this Door County group did with their 1916 Reo.

Changing a tire in 1913 meant jacking up the car, removing the tire from the rim, taking out the tube, applying a tire patch, replacing the tube, and remounting the tire—a job that required the better part of an hour and a half, and took a lot of the fun out of driving.

Ever since man learned to walk upright, he has yearned to fly. Latter-day Icaruses tried two major avenues in their search for a route to the sky. Some concentrated on lighter-than-air craft like balloons and dirigibles; others persisted in their belief that heavier-than-air craft could be made to soar aloft. Working first with kites and then with gliders, members of the second group developed and refined the basic principles of modern aircraft design. The Wright brothers built their first glider in 1900, but Milwaukeeans like these were still trying to fly them a decade later. The result of this particular Packard-powered effort is unknown, but by 1912, biplanes were buzzing through the sky over the incredulous crowd at the Milwaukee Air Show, and a new era in transportation had begun.

City Sidewalks

IN 1855, Silas Chapman of Milwaukee published the second edition of his *Hand Book of Wisconsin*. The purpose of his book was "to represent our prosperous State as it is, and to set up one milestone, from which to measure our future progress." Chapman described, for the benefit of the reader, many Wisconsin cities, and stressed their prosperity and promise:

"Racine is the County Seat, and the Lake port, beautifully located at the mouth of the Root River, which the enterprise of its citizens have converted into a good harbor.

"Appleton is situated on the Fox River, in the very heart of the most beautiful, healthful, fertile and rapidly settling portion of the Fox River Valley. ... Its manufacturing, mechanical and mercantile business already exceeds a quarter of a million of dollars per year. ... Its public schools would reflect honor on many an older town. The population is chiefly American, and is noted throughout the west for Temperance, Morality, Intelligence and Enterprise.

"Milwaukee, the County Seat, is the largest city in the State, and through this port a great part of the exports and imports pass. ... No place in the west has combined so completely, healthiness of location, abundant water power, facilities of manufacture, and equal agricultural lands in its immediate vicinity.

"The village of La Crosse is situated on a high, rolling, and somewhat broken prairie. ... The place, like many others in the State, lacks a good hotel, and if there ever be another, we are sure travelers will avoid the Mississippi House, at least if they are desirous of decent treatment.

"Madison is one of those examples of rapid and continual growth not always found, even in a rapidly increasing State. It is one of the most beautifully located places in the State, between two lakes. ... Besides the Public Edifices alluded to above [the Capitol, the University, the State Lunatic Asylum, and a spa], it has a Female Seminary ... six churches; and what, we regret, is not found in every place in Wisconsin , a good hotel."

By 1920, many of Chapman's provincial Wisconsin towns had become bustling cities. Boardwalks gave way to city sidewalks, and horse-drawn streetcars were replaced by electric trolleys and automobiles. Hotels, factories, and cathedrals rose above the city skyline, and wealthy bankers, lumbermen, and industrialists built elaborate gingerbread mansions. The camera's eye recorded that transformation.

In 1900, Milwaukee's Grand Avenue (now Wisconsin Avenue) was jammed with trolleys, horseless carriages, horse-drawn wagons, and crowds of pedestrians.

A familiar Madison landmark in 1890
was the large water tower on East Washington
Avenue. On market days, crowds of farmers
and shoppers converged on the area to buy
and sell produce and discuss the latest political
and social events. The *Amerika* office at right
housed a prominent Norwegian-American
newspaper. By 1890, Madison boasted of
many municipal improvements: telephones,
electric lights, waterworks, free mail-delivery,
and mule-drawn streetcars.

In 1910, Milwaukee was a bustling industrial
center that still had lots of room for
the small businessman. Milwaukee was
virtually a European town—three-fourths
of the populace either were immigrants or
had at least one foreign-born parent.
That year, Austrian-born Socialist
Victor Berger was elected to Congress
by Milwaukee voters, who also chose
Emil Seidel as the first Socialist
mayor of a major American city.

Two little Milwaukee girls, protected from the cold by long stockings and a woolly muff, posed for a photograph in about 1914. All Saints' Cathedral, completed in 1853, is in the background.

Although rural homemakers baked bread, cakes, and pies at home in their ornate cast-iron stoves, bakers' wagons became a common sight in cities. Crowell's Home Bakery made daily rounds in Oshkosh about 1912, delivering baked goods, ice cream, and confections for the convenience of local housewives.

Oak's Candy Store in Oshkosh at the turn of the century displayed an irresistible assortment of mouth-watering sweets. A nickel bought a whole sackful of goodies— licorice, tangy peppermint sticks, rock candy, chocolate drops, toffee, and nonpareils. Wisconsin already was famous for two confectionary inventions: the ice-cream sundae, first consumed in Two Rivers in 1881; and the malted milk, concocted by William Horlick of Racine in 1883.

State Street in Madison connects what William Ellery Leonard called "the twin domes of law and learning." This view from the Capitol, looking towards the University of Wisconsin, was taken several years before the Bascom Hall dome burned in 1916. During the administration of President Charles R. Van Hise (1903-1918), the university became known nationally for its services to the people of Wisconsin through the University Extension and for the participation of university experts in state government.

The Milwaukee waterfront was the place to see and be seen in 1912. Promenaders rested near the statue of Solomon Juneau, the founder of Milwaukee; strolled past the Cudahy Apartments, behind the statue; and checked the time on the Chicago and North Western Railroad depot's clock. A mile of smooth terraces extended north along Lake Michigan from East Wisconsin Avenue on land once owned by Juneau himself.

A battalion of postal clerks marched in a parade on Grand Avenue in Milwaukee about 1905, when the glorious Fourth of July was celebrated by young and old with parades, picnics, fervent speeches, and fireworks. Just seven years before, the ebullient, aggressive, and fiercely nationalistic United States had jumped into "a splendid little war," one in which newspaper headlines screamed "Remember the *Maine*"; an admiral ordered, "You can fire when you are ready, Gridley"; and a message was carried to Garcia.

Young men took their best girls canoeing on the Milwaukee River in 1912. Shirtwaists—richly tucked and trimmed blouses—were still the height of fashion, as were lavishly flowered and plumed hats. And elegantly dressed ladies apparently demanded fancy canoes—note the padded backrests and the tasseled pillows.

The Milwaukee Electrical Railway and Light Company sponsored an elaborate company outing every summer, like this one in August 1906. Workers and their families climbed aboard a special excursion train bound for Waukesha Beach, where baseball games and ladies' footraces were organized, and gallons of lemonade were consumed.

113

Before the days of refrigerators, ice harvesting was big business in Milwaukee. One company employed 1,000 men each winter to saw off rectangular blocks of ice, float them to the warehouse, and pack them between layers of sawdust and marsh hay. When local warehouses were full, freight trains were loaded with ice blocks to be shipped as far away as New Orleans. The Wisconsin Lakes Ice Company of Milwaukee boasted that all its ice was cut from "clear spring water lakes having no swamps or morasses and whose water contains the proper ingredients for the conservation of the health of the people."

This veneer dryer at the Paine Lumber Company in Oshkosh employed several women in 1903. Wolf River timber was driven to Oshkosh, which became the world's leading sash- and door-producing center. Lumbermen amassed fortunes, and Oshkosh was known as "Sawdust City."

Everyone in the crowd held his breath as a daredevil driver swooped down the ramp, did a graceful loop-the-loop, and then made a four-point landing on a heavy wooden platform supported by enormous springs. This death-defying act, performed at state fairs across the country, was photographed in 1906. The stoic lady in midair, whose name and fate are unknown, was one of a handful of women who attempted the dangerous stunt.

President William H. Taft reviewed the Holstein cattle in the stock parade at the Wisconsin State Fair on September 17, 1909. The locomotives in the infield are set up for a popular fair event in which the two engines backed off, built up a head of steam, and then smashed into each other at full tilt. This early version of the demolition derby was a much-advertised spectacle and a crowd pleaser for a number of years in the early 1900s.

Stark spires of stone marked the Elbridge G. Huggins marble works on Fifth Street in Racine in 1880, when Racine was a bustling lake port with a population of 16,000, including many Bohemian and Scandinavian immigrants.

118

Henry Hamilton Bennett photographed Milwaukee in the days when sailing ships graced the Milwaukee River. By 1875, lake commerce and the extension of railroads into the hinterlands made the city a booming marketplace. This photograph was taken from the Grand Avenue bridge.

If the city was a place of fearsome bigness and bustle to small children, it was also a treasury of exciting places to explore and new things to do. Every park was a playground for children at the turn of the century. Photographed as they frolicked near an elaborate splashing fountain are two little girls, dressed in their everyday smocks and long cotton stockings.

Two sober-faced children posed for a photographer in about 1893. To have their formal portrait made, they were dressed in their finest clothes and carefully positioned against an "artistic" backdrop. These two remarkable children—neither even blinked while the photograph was taken— are Vera E. Davidson, aged four, and her little brother, Leo, aged one.

Youngsters were dwarfed by Exposition Hall, built by Milwaukee merchants and industrialists in 1879 at a cost of $200,000. Topped by a polygonal dome 175 feet high, the fantastic structure burned down during the American Skat Congress in 1905, disrupting the card games. The Arena-Auditorium occupies the site today.

Growing populations unfortunately meant an increase in crime, and city police departments needed sophisticated equipment and techniques. Part of the Oshkosh police force took a breather from catching crooks and posed for their portrait in 1920. Officer Tony Ilk is at the wheel of the paddy wagon.

Firemen tested their equipment in Milwaukee in 1900. Preparedness was important, for Milwaukee had suffered several disastrous fires in the nineteenth century. Sixty-four persons were known to have perished in the Newhall House fire in 1883 (the famous midget Tom Thumb and his wife were saved), and nine years later, a conflagration destroyed sixteen blocks of business and residential districts between the Milwaukee River and Lake Michigan.

These nattily attired young men sauntered past the Joseph Schlitz Brewing Company in Milwaukee just after the turn of the century. Horse-drawn streetcars had not yet been replaced by electric trolleys on this street.

Managing the large, beribboned hats that were stylish in 1912 was difficult on a gusty day. Many proper women thought twice before venturing into a wind that would mold their garments to their limbs. Walking was made even more hazardous by "hobble" skirts, which allowed only a very short step. This candid scene was photographed in downtown Milwaukee.

In the 1890s, before the days of bottled beer, a neighborhood often chipped in to buy a barrel of beer, and each family siphoned out its share. This method of obtaining beer was known as "rushing the growler." In many Milwaukee industries, beer for the morning and afternoon "beer breaks" was procured by sending a bucket boy to the nearest saloon.

Milwaukeeans spent many a genial summer afternoon at Pabst's Whitefish Bay Resort, where *Gemütlichkeit* prevailed. The beer garden opened in 1889 and closed in 1914. During those years, patrons could reach the resort either by boarding a Lake Michigan steamer near the Wisconsin Avenue bridge or, until 1898, by taking a seat on the Milwaukee and Whitefish Bay Railroad. This photograph was made on August 23, 1897.

Especially for Wisconsinites of Teutonic heritage, beer drinking was a social custom and the saloon was a community center. Men gathered there for a couple of steins of beer, friendly conversation with their peers, plus several amenities not usually associated with today's taverns. At Tom Ryan's Bar on Main Street in Oshkosh in 1912, you could get your shoes shined while you discussed Woodrow Wilson's campaign for president. Many saloons featured a generous free meal. Fred Holmes told of four saloons in Milwaukee in the 1890s that "sold two beers for a nickel and provided an elaborate free lunch of roast beef, baked ham, sausage, baked beans, vegetables, salads, bread and butter, and other appetizing foods. Two men with but a nickel between them could each enjoy a substantial meal and a mammoth beer."

Led by such stars as "Sleepy" Smith (standing, second from right), catcher George Redempto (standing, far right), and pitcher James Wood (seated, far left), Milwaukee's Cream City Baseball Club won the state championship in 1868. The team, photographed in 1869, went on to defeat the Cincinnati Red Stockings in 1870 and joined the National League in 1878.

Milwaukee baseball was back in the minor leagues in 1909, but the Milwaukee-Minneapolis game drew a sellout crowd on September 17. Brewer fans paid a quarter to sit on the wooden bleachers at Borchert Field. Major-league baseball didn't return to Milwaukee until 1953.

A Life of Leisure

IN THE FIRST ISSUE of *Atlantic Monthly*, in 1858, a contributor wondered, "Who in this community really takes exercise? Even the mechanic confines himself to one set of muscles; the blacksmith acquires strength in his right arm, and the dancing teacher in his left leg. But the professional or business man, what muscles has he at all?"

Early Wisconsin settlers gave precious little time to amusement and exercise—merely to exist taxed every resource. But once the need for incessant labor diminished, a desire for companionship and fun arose out of their hard and often lonely lives. At first, work and pleasure were combined. Hunting and fishing, barn raisings and husking bees, spelling bees and debates, all provided opportunities to socialize and have fun while accomplishing something useful.

By the end of the nineteenth century—aided by such revolutionary changes as the ten-hour day, Saturday half-holidays, and the two-week summer vacation—Wisconsinites had begun to discover the joy and exhilaration of leisure-time activity and vigorous exercise, and organized recreation came into its own.

Nearly all of today's most popular spectator sports were founded in the days between the Civil War and the turn of the century. Each new sport was adopted with wholehearted enthusiasm. Baseball teams, each with a wildly partisan cheering section, sprang up in every small town, and by 1872, *Sports and Games* magazine acclaimed baseball "the national game of the United States." Basketball—first played with nine-man teams and peach baskets for goals—drew crowds of excited fans in the 1890s.

Along with the phenomenal popularity of spectator sports, a series of athletics crazes swept the country. Croquet was a virtual epidemic that began on fashionable lawns in the East and went west with the homesteaders—some sets were even made with candle sockets on the wickets for night playing. And roller skating was the rage in the 1880s, especially after smooth-running metal wheels replaced the wooden-spool rollers that had often broken with disastrous results.

Archery, lawn tennis, and golf were genteel sports that could be enjoyed by both sexes. Gymnastics clubs (*Turnverein* in German communities), rowing clubs, and bowling teams were organized. But bicycling was the most spectacular craze of all. Ladies eagerly participated in this "step toward the emancipation of woman," and *Outing* magazine confidently announced that "Bicycling is a fraternity of more permanent organization than ever characterized any sport since the world began." There was, as well, a great return to the out-of-doors, as long-distance hikes, mountain climbing, and canoeing gained enthusiastic adherents.

Even for the less athletic, there were broad horizons in recreation. Excursions on steamboats (which advertised special rates for photographers), summer resorts, dances, and card parties were popular. Circuses and traveling theatrical companies entertained thousands. Not to be outdone, or ignored, churches and schools organized literary societies, box socials, raffles, and even drama groups. They were sometimes disguised as "moral uplift" activities, but most often they contributed to the life of leisure most Wisconsinites were beginning to enjoy.

Carriage traffic on the Main Street bridge in Oshkosh was brisk in the 1890s. And business at Captain Charles Dunkel's boat livery was good, for sailing on Lake Winnebago in the Gay Nineties was as popular as it is today, if a bit more sedate. The captain manufactured and rented rowboats, sailboats, skiffs, and canoes.

"Mud shows" traveled from town to town in horse-drawn wagons on dirt roads that could become quagmires after an hour's rain. The elephants always traveled at the rear, ready to pull out wagons that became mired. This was the George W. Hall Show out of Evansville in 1911.

Wisconsin—Mother of Circuses

Wisconsin had a circus before she had statehood, and by the time the last native show closed in 1938, some 100 circuses had been born in Wisconsin. Some were mud shows or dog and pony shows, but there were big names too—the seven Ringling Brothers, the Mabie Brothers, the five Gollmars, the Lindemans, Burr Robbins, William C. Coup, and others. Delavan alone was home to twenty-six circuses, but many small towns had at least one claim to fame—the Holloway Brothers Circus out of Birnamwood, Skerbeck's Circus out of Dorchester, Dode Fisk Shows from Wonewoc, and Bugler and Chaney Railroad Shows out of Sparta. It's a glorious heritage of daring trapeze artists and spangled ladies, foolhardy lion-tamers and tumbling clowns.

At one time, the five Gollmar Brothers' "Great United Shows: Circus, Menagerie, and Congress of Trained Animals" from Baraboo was the third-largest circus in the country. This is how their troupe looked in 1892.

Advance men, masters of hyperbole, plastered every flat surface they could find with brilliantly colored posters designed to enthrall young and old, like one advertising "The Burr Robbins New Consolidated Railroad Shows, A Syndicate of Bewildering Amusements, Grecian Circus, Colossal Hippodrome, and Oriental Caravan." And the promise of "Popcorn George" Hall's poster rang true: "The amusement lov-ing public is fickle, but never for an instant does it lose its faith in the blare of the band, the clashing of cymbals, the shrill piping of fifes, the roars of the lions, the rumble of the heavy-loaded red wagons, the smell of sawdust and the shout of merry old clowns."

Street scenes like this one were commonplace in towns throughout Wisconsin. The Ringling elephant herd shuffling through Baraboo in 1904 on its daily exercise route drew an excited bunch of small boys. Every spring, usually in April, the circus was loaded on flatcars, and headed out of town for its season's tour.

Clown costumes and grease paint overflowed wardrobe trunks in the clowns' dressing room of the 1897 Ringling Brothers Circus troupe. Soon the shrill piping of the steam calliope would announce the beginning of the matinee show, and baggy-suited clowns would somersault gaily into the main ring.

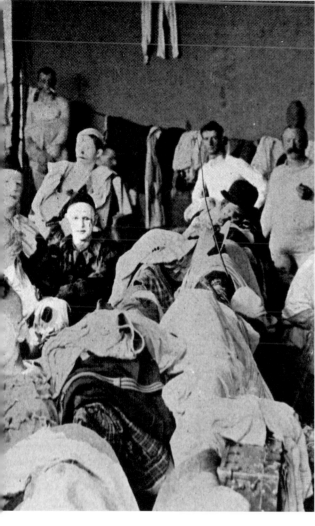

The band played a military march, wagons flew banners and flags, big draft horses wore plumes in their bridles, beautiful ladies in bright but modest costumes rode sidesaddle, clowns tumbled along the way, and elaborate parade wagons gleamed in the sun. This was a Ringling Brothers Circus parade in Milwaukee about 1890.

"Tiger of the waters—and justly does the muskellunge deserve this name. It is the largest and most coveted prize of the fresh-water angler. They are wily beyond imagination and when hooked it requires skill and fast thinking to bring them to gaff." Thus gushed an early northern-Wisconsin tourist guide. This formally attired angler, A. A. Bish, caught this "muskalonge" from an equally formal steam launch on Long Lake in Chippewa County in August 1894.

In 1900, these eight doughty deer-slayers and their hound displayed the results of a very successful hunt—six bucks, eleven does, and one unidentified pelt. In those days, tents and supplies were packed in horse-drawn wagons and thousands of hunters took to the bush for a couple of weeks of roughing it. It was sport, and a chance to get away with the boys, but venison was a necessary supplement to the larder of many Wisconsin families.

During the heyday of duck hunting around the turn of the century, spring hunting and live decoys were legal. Market hunters with cannonlike punt guns mounted on flatboats could kill 100 birds with a single shot, and they sent ducks by the barrel to famous restaurants in Eastern cities as far away as New York. It must have seemed to these three Winnebago County duck hunters with their bag of more than 300 birds that ducks would always sweep across the sky in unlimited numbers. But of course, they were wrong.

This dapper group is posing with their bag on a Wolf River steamboat. Those were the days (circa 1912) when a party of hunters could board a steamer in town and be carried in style upstream to the hunting grounds.

Headquarters for many duck hunters along the wild-rice-choked lower Wolf River were floating shanties like these. Very likely, the first ones were wanigans discarded after the spring log-drives and converted into sleeping and cooking quarters for the hunters.

A play-reading group gathered in Black River Falls in 1893. The men are urbane; the ladies, stylish—particularly the two who are dressed to the hilt in their newly fashionable leg-o'-mutton sleeves. Shakespeare, of course, was always popular fare, along with more contemporary works like *The Pride of the West*, *East Lynne*, and that perennial tear-jerker, *Uncle Tom's Cabin*.

The town band was noted not so much for the quality of its music as for the cut of its uniforms. Bands and their music were a very important part of life in Wisconsin communities. They paraded on every holiday, and sometimes they even gave impromptu concerts in the street. These are the musicians of the Herman Band, which played for Sheboygan audiences in 1871. One can almost hear the hearty polkas and schottisches and the concerts in the bandstand on warm summer evenings.

Every spring, burly lumberjacks rode bucking log rafts through the gap in the Kilbourn Dam near what is now Wisconsin Dells. These young ladies of 1888, however, were whiling away an afternoon in the less strenuous activity of skipping pebbles across the Wisconsin River.

Chautauqua was an annual summer educational and recreational assembly. It began in New York in the 1870s as a camp-meeting course for Sunday-school teachers. By 1920, 10,000 Chautauquas were held all across the country. The meeting lasted for a solid week, and hundreds of farm families and townspeople came to camp on nearby grounds to hear lectures, both learned and inspirational, and to enjoy entertainment that ranged from glee clubs and dramatic monologues to boy whistlers, jugglers, and jubilee singers. A violin solo at the Racine Chautauqua in 1906 drew an attentive crowd. Just outside, the Women's Christian Temperance Union had erected a large tent as headquarters for their own particular brand of moral uplift.

RACINE CHAUTAUQUA '06

332

BISHOP

The moccasin game was a favorite with the Ho-Chunk Indians. Two equal teams opposed each other. A small object, often a lead bullet, was placed in the moccasin of one team member. The other side then attempted to guess which moccasin held the bullet. The guesser, who held a long stick to turn over the proper moccasin, carefully scrutinized the expression of each opponent. The players on his side sang songs and made remarks attempting to catch off-guard the man whose moccasin contained the bullet. These Ho-Chunks were playing moccasin near Kilbourn in the late 1880s.

It was a man's world in 1910 when this jaunty group of gentlemen enjoyed a stag outing on a pleasant summer's day. There was good masculine conversation, a couple of barrels of beer, a picnic lunch, and a guitar, should they be taken with the urge to harmonize a popular song or two. In this era, the woman's place still was strictly in the home, while business, politics, and the professions were the exclusive province of the man.

During the horse-and-buggy days, harness racing reached its zenith. There was the legendary stallion Hambletonian, who, by the time he died in 1876, had sired 1,331 foals, many of whom became famous trotters noted for their speed and stamina. And there was the storied Dan Patch, who ran thirty two-minute miles, more than any other trotter. This harness race was held during the Inter-City Fair near Kilbourn in 1905.

An ice-boat fleet was poised to begin a race on Lake Mendota in Madison in 1910. William P. Bernard of Madison pioneered in designing the streamlined racing craft, and his innovations in balance and design culminated in the Princess II, which won the international ice-boating cup in 1914 and defended it successfully for eighteen years. Bernard and his sons, Paul and Carl, made Madison the capital of the cold world of ice boating, and brought the swift sport a long way from the winter of 1854-55, when crude triangular platforms on runners had been used to transport building materials across frozen Lake Mendota.

Cutting graceful figures on the Town Club rink in Milwaukee in about 1915 were these four couples. In addition to private rinks, every winter the frozen Milwaukee River became a skater's delight, offering long, inviting stretches of smooth ice for latter-day Hans Brinkers.

In summer, the Milwaukee waterfront was a haven from the heat, and a pleasant place to bring the children on a June afternoon. In 1915, men could swim in relative comfort in cotton shirts and knee pants, but women were weighed down by bathing costumes that included a short-sleeved blouse, calf-length skirt, bloomers, cotton stockings, and a duster cap. Just two years before, a woman swimmer in Atlantic City had been fiercely pelted with sand and epithets by the local guardians of decency, who considered her bathing suit too short.

The determination and dash of these modestly attired ladies, shown in a footrace at the Milwaukee Electrical Railway and Light Company employees' outing at Waukesha Beach in the summer of 1908, was the result of changing times and changing fashions. While these ladies certainly are adequately clothed, by this time women had been liberated from the tyranny of corsets, and were beginning to throw themselves into sports of all kinds with gusto.

"There is no truth more firmly established among medical men than that disease follows fashion as much as bonnets do," wrote Lyman Draper in 1870. "The reign of corsets is denoted by collapsed lungs, dyspepsia, and a general derangement of the digestive organs. So intimately are dress and disease connected, that a doctor says that all he needs to determine what a majority of the women are dying of, is to have an inventory of their wardrobe." But physicians were not the only ones encouraging women to adopt a freer physical and intellectual life. Famed modern dancer Isadora Duncan was another. With costumes that allowed unfettered and expressive motion, these disciples of the glamorous Isadora performed in 1915.

Lawn tennis was introduced to the United States by Miss Mary Outerbridge in 1874. Though the game spread rapidly throughout the country, it was still considered a sissy sport by nonplayers, especially men, at the time this couple engaged in a set of mixed doubles just after the turn of the century. The prospect of grown men patting a ball back and forth and shouting "love" to one another was more than the average man could stand. Note the lady's cumbersome tennis dress and her choked grip on the racquet.

The scenic wonders of the Wisconsin River dells were depicted and made famous by local photographer H. H. Bennett. And when tourists converged on the area to experience the natural beauty by train, boat, and even trolley, Bennett was there to provide a permanent reminder of their visit. This group of travelers paused for his camera before the trim little side-wheeler, *Alexander Mitchell*, set off upstream through the "narrows" on the way to Witches' Gulch and Cold Water Canyon in the mid-1880s.

Some of the earliest excursions to see the scenic dells of the Wisconsin River were made in rowboats like these. A perfect Sunday outing in the 1880s included gentlemen dressed to the nines in serge suits and top hats; genteel, fair-complexioned ladies protected from the burning rays of the sun by parasols; and the wild beauty of the Wisconsin River's most famous stretch.

The Fabric of Life

COMMON THREADS ran through the lives of all Wisconsinites—immigrant or native-born, black or white, man or woman, rich or poor, farmer or city dweller—weaving their disparate situations into one common experience. Social institutions like courtship and marriage, birth and death, politics, military life, religion, and education joined people with differing heritages, and gave their lives a distinctive Wisconsin pattern.

It was in the schoolroom, more than anywhere else, that these diverse traditions were interwoven, though as late as 1890 a bill requiring the teaching of English in all state schools was so bitterly opposed that the Republicans responsible for passing it were swept out of office to a man. The first kindergarten in the country was organized by Mrs. Carl Schurz in Watertown in 1855, and Wisconsin also led the United States in vocational training, opening the first such school in Racine in 1911.

By that time, the University of Wisconsin, which had been founded in 1848, already enjoyed a national reputation for excellence, and the board of regents had uttered its now-famous statement in defense of educational freedom: "Whatever may be the limitations which trammel inquiry elsewhere, we believe that the great state University of Wisconsin should ever encourage that continual and fearless sifting and winnowing by which alone the truth can be found."

For many young men, the completion of their education meant the beginning of their military service. Cameras were just beginning to capture Wisconsin scenes when Fort Sumter fell and President Lincoln called for 75,000 volunteers. Within a week, thirty-six Wisconsin companies had stepped forward. Enthusiasm for the war soon cooled, however; later quotas had to be met by drafts, and violent anticonscription riots broke out in German communities around Port Washington. In all, the war claimed the lives of over 12,000 Wisconsin men, including Governor Louis Harvey, who drowned on a relief mission to Wisconsin troops in 1862. The Spanish-American War, Mexican Border service, and World War I lengthened the list of Wisconsinites who died defending their country and its policies.

As early as 1851, the special vitality of Wisconsin political life had been noted by Samuel Freeman: "Wisconsin gives you a voice in choosing Representatives to serve you in her councils. Preserve this treasure as you would your life. Here you will see men who strive for the removal of defects in the existing order of things, and suggest social and political projects for ameliorating the condition of their fellow-men."

The Republican party was born at Ripon in 1854, and by 1880 a young man named Robert La Follette was spearheading a reform wing within the organization. Elected governor three times, La Follette led the Progressives to new heights in social legislation, including a civil service act and a railroad regulation bill. La Follette was elected to the United States Senate in 1906, but his Progressive party adopted a less popular provision in 1911—the income tax. Meanwhile, Milwaukee was giving birth to the nation's most successful Socialist movement. By 1910, the Socialists had captured nearly all the city and county offices, elected twelve assemblymen and two senators to the state legislature, and sent the first Socialist to the United States Congress. And shortly afterward, in 1920, Wisconsin became the first state in the country to ratify the amendment allowing women to vote.

Vital as life in Wisconsin was between the Civil War and the Roaring Twenties, it was not without the shadow of sickness and death. But as military surgeons returned from the Civil War, as anesthesia was discovered, and as the true causes of diseases like malaria and cholera were determined, the time of the pioneer doctor who bravely faced the wilderness—and the pioneer who bravely faced the doctor—came to an end. The people of Wisconsin entered the modern era with a new confidence in themselves and in the future of their state.

In the mid-1600s an explorer described the Ho-Chunk like this: "These savages are naturally very impatient of control, and very passionate; they are great braggarts. They are, however, well-built, and are brave soldiers, who do not know what danger is. They cannot be humble. Their women are extremely laborious, and are neat in their houses." In this photograph of Alex Lonetree and his family, the women are wearing modern clothing, but the men are dressed more traditionally in leggings and garters; beaded shirts, belts, and moccasins; and shell gorgets and beaded collars.

153

This Ho-Chunk woman was photographed tanning a hide at an encampment near Wisconsin Dells in the mid-1800s. Tanning, like the building of the lodges seen in the background, was women's work. First the hair was scraped from the skin. Next the skin was stretched on an upright frame, and all traces of flesh were removed. Then the hide was soaked in a mixture of deer brains and water, followed by a thorough washing. Finally, the skin was dried and smoked over a wood fire.

This is Betsy Thunder, respected Ho-Chunk herbalist and doctor from the Black River Falls area, resplendent in a traditional appliquéd skirt and beautifully beaded moccasins and leggings. Though their concept of disease was quite different from that of white physicians, many Indian doctors were both knowledgeable and effective. Herbalists knew the medicinal effects many plants had on the human body and administered their concoctions liberally. Occasionally, it was a question of which would succumb first—the symptoms or the sick man— but, like Betsy, some Indian doctors gained such renown for their healing skills that they numbered white settlers among their patients.

Lewis Hughes also wanted to preserve his heritage. A former slave who had escaped to become a professional nurse in Milwaukee, he published his autobiography in 1897. It was called *Thirty Years A Slave*. Hughes believed that "the enlightenment of each generation depends upon the thoughtful study of the history of those who have gone before," and recorded his experiences with the help of his daughter Lydia, a college graduate. The 210-page volume can be found in the Milwaukee Public Library.

By 1856, Indian title to Wisconsin lands covered only a few reservations, and many Wisconsin Indians were removed to land west of the Mississippi. These students at the Hayward Indian School in about 1885 symbolize the official government policy toward Indians—assimilation.

Only a few students were present when the traveling photographer visited Halcyon School near Black River Falls in the early 1890s. Tardiness and absence were the rule in rural areas. Prudent communities hired a man to teach for the winter months, when the rowdy farm boys were free to come to school, and retained a woman for the spring term, when the class usually was made up mostly of girls.

School was not all drudgery and rote learning. Friday afternoons often were given over to contests in the classroom—spelling bees, ciphering competitions, and geography games. On the last day of school in spring, students and their families eagerly made their way to a nearby woods for the annual school picnic. While the women spread out a lunch in the shade, the men and boys organized a baseball game, and the children went wading in the creek. The students of Shamrock School near Black River Falls assumed a more scholarly appearance for this photograph, taken about 1893.

Until well after 1900, most country schools were ungraded, and each scholar worked at his own pace through standards like McGuffey's reader, Webster's speller, Ray's arithmetic, and the Eclectic history and geography. The "loud school," where every pupil studied at the top of his lungs, was out of vogue. But in the "quiet school" that succeeded it, reported historian Fred Shannon, "the scratching of slate pencils, snapping of fingers, clattering of cowhide boot heels or copper toeplates, and the rattling of the dipper in the bucket, as water was passed around the room, prevented silence from becoming too oppressive." These youngsters attended Van Dyne School in Fond du Lac County in 1905.

At recess time, everyone raced outside to play drop the handkerchief, fox and geese, pom pom pull-away, or another popular game. When the school bell rang at the end of recess, the children trooped back into the schoolhouse for more of the three R's. Intent on their game of drop the handkerchief are students at the Howlett School in Black Wolf near Oshkosh in 1902.

Wisconsin's first normal school opened at Platteville in 1866, and by 1900 at least six more had been established. These schools, along with many private academies, trained teachers for elementary and secondary schools. Training in janitorial work would also have been useful, for most teachers had to come to the schoolhouse early to unlock the door, carry in wood and water, and kindle the fire. On Washington Island in 1912, teachers Mabel Robinson and Gertrude Klumb found that skiing was the easiest way to reach their classroom.

Young ladies attending Downer College in Fox Lake spent hours in the biology laboratory, where they were able to study anatomy, botany, and many other branches of natural science under the watchful eye in the cupboard. This photograph was taken a short time before Downer College merged with Milwaukee College in 1895 to form Milwaukee-Downer College, a private, liberal-arts school for women. Another merger, nearly seventy years later, would see Milwaukee-Downer become part of Lawrence University in Appleton.

Speaking of the University of Wisconsin in his book, *Story of My Boyhood and Youth*, Wisconsin-born naturalist John Muir wrote: "No University, it seemed to me, could be more admirably situated, and as I sauntered about it, charmed with its fine lawns and trees and beautiful lakes, and saw the students going and coming with their books, and occasionally practicing with a theodolite in measuring distances, I thought that if I could only join them it would be the greatest joy of life. I was desperately hungry and thirsty for knowledge and willing to endure anything to get it.

"One day I chanced to meet a student who... recognized me. And when I said, 'You are fortunate fellows to be allowed to study in this beautiful place. I wish I could join you.' 'Well, why don't you?' he asked. 'I haven't any money,' I said. 'Oh, as to money,' he reassuringly explained, 'very little is required. I presume you're able to enter the Freshman class, and you can board yourself as quite a number of us do at a cost of about a dollar a week. The baker and milk-man come every day. You can live on bread and milk.' Well, I thought, maybe I have money enough for at least one beginning term. Anyhow I couldn't help trying."

The furnishings of a student's room at the University of Wisconsin reveal much about the student of 1899. Posters and banners, family photographs, and military drill equipment adorned the walls, a dance program hung from the dresser, and a likeness of a sweetheart was propped on this scholar's desk.

Candy and romance seemed to go together in the 1890s. When a young man came to call on his girl, almost invariably he appeared in the front parlor with a box of bonbons. Even so, courting couples frequently retired to the kitchen to make fudge or pull taffy. A group of friends at the University of Wisconsin held this fudge party in about 1890.

This handsome group is the University of Wisconsin's 1901 freshman crew, sans crew cuts. Situated on the shore of Lake Mendota, the university was, and is, one of a few Midwestern schools to sponsor crew. The oarsmen usually had to travel to Eastern colleges in order to find any competition.

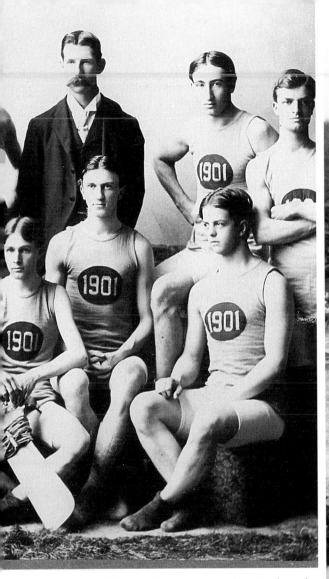

Class rush was an annual spectacle at the University of Wisconsin from about 1908 to 1923. The contest between the freshman and sophomore classes was held at various locations on campus, and on some occasions overflowed into Lake Mendota. This photograph was taken on the lower campus in 1919. The two opposing classes faced each other across a large playing field. At a signal, each group rushed forward and tried to capture as many of the large flour sacks in the center as possible, and then dragged the sacks across the opposing team's starting line. The class with the most sacks won. After the contest, teams and spectators joined in a friendly, noisy parade up State Street.

All the ten o'clock scholars of Wrolstead School in Iola, plus their proud parents, gathered before their tidy little schoolhouse in the 1890s. The occasion may have been spring commencement activities, for the little girls are wearing their most ruffly dresses, and the small boys are properly (and unwillingly, by their expressions) turned out in starchy white collars.

In rural Wisconsin, the rare pupil who wanted to study beyond the "sixth reader"—roughly eight grades—had to move to a large town to find a high school. Arthur Weber was one such student. He left his parents' farm near Forestville to board with a family and attend school in Sturgeon Bay. High-school graduation was an important event in 1907. As valedictorian of his class of twelve, Arthur gave an address. There was also a speech by Professor Hohlfeld, a class play, piano and vocal solos, a concert by the mandolin orchestra, and a presentation of dictionaries, along with the awarding of diplomas. The proud parents ordered a formal portrait of the graduate, but to get their money's worth, they threw in Arthur's kid brother Clarence.

But if a high-school diploma was something special in the early 1900s, a college degree was a rare and coveted treasure. Elaborate graduation ceremonies at the University of Wisconsin began in mid-May with the annual May Fete, a celebration held on Bascom Hill and shown here in about 1917. Under the benign gaze of Abraham Lincoln and numerous relatives and friends, an intricate web of streamers was slowly and gracefully woven tight to the Maypoles in a scene that's hard to imagine on Bascom Hill today.

Civil War veteran Captain J.N.P. Bird of Wautoma sat for a portrait shortly after the war. In 1862, his company had presented him with a testimonial of their appreciation—a beautifully engraved sword and scabbard with a sash and belt, all proudly displayed in the photograph. A popular and effective commanding officer, Captain Bird returned to Wautoma after the war, where he served in public office until his death in 1886.

Towering bluffs stood sentinel at Camp Philip Reade, just north of the village of Camp Douglas, about 1900. The first military use of the area took place in September 1888, when a rifle camp was held on the 400-acre site, which had been purchased earlier that year by General Chandler P. Chapman, State Adjutant. The property was turned over to the state in 1889, and over the years additional land was acquired in honor of Lieutenant-Colonel Charles R. Williams. By then, the days of circular field tents and gallant horse cavalry were past.

Decoration day in Oshkosh on May 31, 1886, brought hundreds to memorial services in the cemetery. Civil War veterans wore their medals, and little boys and girls solemnly beat on drums. In attendance were Post Number Ten of the Grand Army of the Republic (G.A.R.), the G.A.R. Drum Corps and Juvenile Drum Corps, Companies B and F of the Second Regiment of the Wisconsin National Guard, and the patriotic citizenry of Oshkosh.

In 1900, a rumpled but silver-tongued William Jennings Bryan spoke in Columbus as he campaigned for the presidency on the Democratic ticket. The "Boy Orator of the Platte" had risen to national prominence at the 1896 Democratic national convention, where his stirring address in favor of free coinage of silver to aid rural America had included the ringing phrase, "You shall not crucify mankind upon a cross of gold." In spite of the attentive crowd he drew here, Bryan, also known as "The Great Commoner," carried neither Wisconsin nor the nation in 1900, and William McKinley was elected President.

Robert M. La Follette Sr. campaigned in Cumberland in 1897. A contemporary of Bryan and also a superb orator, La Follette led the reform faction in Wisconsin's Republican party as it fought bossism and corruption. In 1900, La Follette was elected governor, and under his direction Wisconsin became an outstanding example of progressive government. La Follette helped create the "Wisconsin Idea," which advocated using experts from the University of Wisconsin to serve the state government, and extended the boundaries of the university to the edges of the state. By 1912, largely as a result of La Follette's leadership, Theodore Roosevelt could say that Wisconsin had become "literally a laboratory for wise experimental legislation aiming to serve the social and political betterment of the people as a whole."

Wisconsin's fourth Capitol had been completed in 1869 at a cost of $900,000, and not without much angry opposition from those who preferred merely to enlarge the existing structure. On the night of February 27, 1904, a leaking gas jet on the second floor touched off a fire that quickly engulfed the building. Students, state officials, and townspeople rescued many valuable documents, but the fire gutted three wings. This dramatic view from East Main Street was taken at 4 a.m. by young Joseph Livermore of Madison with his vest-pocket Kodak. Joseph, aged fifteen, did a brisk business selling prints of his photograph at five cents each to finance the purchase of a bicycle. He wanted to charge ten cents apiece, but his father considered that sum exorbitant.

The fifth, and present, Capitol was under construction when this view up State Street from the corner of State and Johnson was taken in 1911. By 1917, the handsome $7,200,000 structure was completed. Designed in the form of a Greek cross, it was crowned with an imposing dome topped by a gold-leafed statue named "Forward." When it was discovered that the original plans called for a building taller than the nation's Capitol in Washington, Wisconsin respectfully lopped several inches off the top of its dome.

Anton DeBack gave up his homeland when he left Rotterdam to come to America, but he found a new life and a wife in Sheboygan. He and Elsie Kruschke had a formal wedding portrait—complete with jaguar rug—made in a Sheboygan studio in 1908.

When Alfred, Lord Tennyson wrote, "In the spring a young man's fancy lightly turns to thoughts of love," he could well have had this couple in mind. Courting, 1913-style, included picking nosegays of marsh flowers. This gallant swain is assisting his lady on a boggy trail near Cedarburg.

The bride and groom, plus all the aunts, uncles, cousins, neighbors, and friends, lined up to pose for the photographer at this country wedding near Iola in the 1890s. In the evening, the guests would reassemble for the shivaree. They would steal to the newlyweds' home. There, shouting and pounding on pans, they would raise an ungodly racket to wake the sleeping couple. Feigning amazement to find anyone there, the bride and groom would invite everyone in for refreshments. The shivaree was a combination wedding reception and housewarming, and put the community's seal of approval on a marriage. A young couple often received forty acres of land—enough for a homestead—as a wedding gift, so soon the friends and relatives would gather again for a gala barn-raising.

White mourning bands were as common as black ones at funerals on the Wisconsin frontier. White was worn at the death of a child and symbolized the infant's innocence. A doctor estimated in the 1880s that over 20 percent of the children died before they reached five years of age, so funerals like this one were common, and tiny headstones decorated with lambs dotted cemeteries across the state. Poor housing, primitive sanitation, and inadequate medical care were the main causes; early marriages and large families, the most common solutions.

In the late 1890s, this Black River Falls man got up from his sickbed to pose with uncommon dignity for what was probably his last portrait. It was not unusual for a photographer to be called to make a final photograph of a dying person. Sometimes, if the death was sudden or the photographer late, the survivors propped the body in a chair to record one last image.

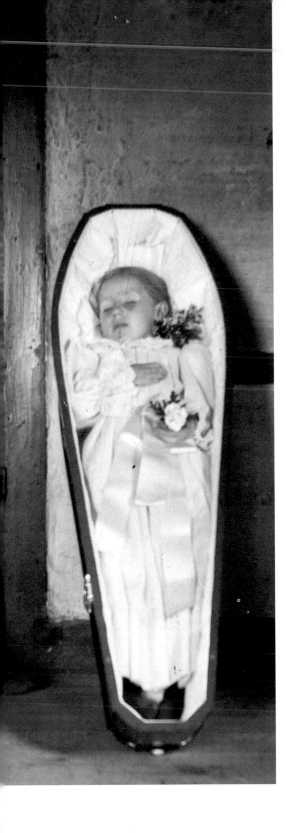

A Ho-Chunk Indian woman and her child were photographed by Henry Hamilton Bennett at Wisconsin Dells about 1880. Wisconsin's Ho-Chunks were but a remnant by that date, but this baby would live to see his people experience a resurgence of population and a rebirth of tradition. His life would intertwine with the lives of countless other nameless Wisconsinites to provide us with a portrait of our past.

Photography Credits

Abbreviations will be used for these photo sources: State Historical Society of Wisconsin (SHSW), Oshkosh Public Museum (OPM), Milwaukee Public Museum (MPM), Milwaukee County Historical Society (MCHS), and H. H. Bennett Studio (HHBS).

Front cover—OPM; back, upper—SHSW (H44)94; center—SHSW (V2/D)796; lower, OPM • Page 4, OPM • Page 4-5, upper—SHSW (V24/D)1706; lower—SHSW (V2/D)168 • Page 7, OPM • Page 8, SHSW • Page 9, SHSW • Page 10, SHSW (D489)9631 • Page 10/11, left—SHSW; right—SHSW (D489) 9620 • Page 12, SHSW (X3)14027 • Page 13, SHSW (B5)266 • Page 14, MPM • Page 15, SHSW (X3)1397 • Page 16, OPM • Page 17, upper—SHSW (X3)14697; lower—MPM • Page 18-19, OPM • Page 20-21, HHBS • Page 23, SHSW (H44)94 • Page 24, SHSW (W6)21131 • Page 25, Virginia Stuebe • Page 26, SHSW (W6)27011 • Page 27, upper—Arthur Weber; lower—SHSW (V2)265 • Page 28, SHSW (X3)25594 • Page 29, MPM • Page 30, OPM • Page 30-31, SHSW (V24/D)2160 • Page 31, SHSW (H44)83 • Page 32 left—SHSW (V24/D)2215; right—OPM • Page 33, OPM • Page 34, upper—Russell; lower—SHSW • Page 35, OPM • Page 36, SHSW • Page 37, OPM • Page 38, SHSW (H44)99 • Page 39, SHSW (V2)156 • Page 40, SHSW (X3)36807 • Page 41, SHSW (V24/D)2033 • Page 42, OPM • Page 43, SHSW (V24/D)2081 • Page 44, left—SHSW (B35)81; upper and lower—OPM • Page 45-46, OPM • Page 47, SHSW (X3)24405 • Page 48, SHSW (W6)19734 • Page 49, OPM • Page 51, SHSW (V2/D)3 • Page 52, SHSW (V2/D)69 • Page 53-54, OPM • Page 54-55, SHSW (V2/D)187 • Page 55, OPM • Page 56, left—SHSW (V2)21; right—SHSW (C3)701 • Page 57, SHSW • Page 58, SHSW (V2/D)757 • Page 59, left—Mr. and Mrs. Victor Hanson; center—Mr. and Mrs. James Stone; right—Mr. and Mrs. Edward Mahnke • Page 60-61, HHBS • Page 62, left—OPM; right—SHSW (V24/D)1696 • Page 63, OPM • Page 64, SHSW (V2)405 • Page 65, SHSW (V24/D)1923 • Page 66, OPM • Page 67 SHSW (V22/D)1250 • Page 68, SHSW (V2)874 • Page 69, upper—OPM; lower—SHSW (X3)24627 • Page 70, OPM • Page 70-71, OPM • Page 71, SHSW (X28)2759 • Page 72, SHSW (X3)25561 • Page 73, HHBS • Page 74, SHSW (G471)15 • Page 75, OPM • Page 77, SHSW (S65)48 • Page 78, MPM • Page 79, left—SHSW (X3)43658; right—SHSW (V22/D)1877 • Page 80, MCHS • Page 81, OPM • Page 82, upper—MCHS; lower—SHSW (X3)14799 • Page 83, Garton Toy Company • Page 84, MCHS • Page 85, MPM • Page 86, SHSW (X3)15465 • Page 87, SHSW (X3)15467 • Page 88, OPM • Page 89, OPM • Page 90, SHSW (X3)1476 • Page 91, OPM • Page 92, SHSW (X3)14821 • Page 93, HHBS • Page 94, left—SHSW (X3)2209; upper—SHSW (X3)1531 • Page 95, SHSW (X3)1748 • Page 96, OPM • Page 97, FWD Corporation • Page 98, Mr. and Mrs. James Stone • Page 98-99, American Motors Corporation • Page 99, SHSW (X3)51640 • Page 100, left—Mrs. Arthur Weber; right—SHSW (X3)25616 • Page 101, OPM • Page 102, MPM • Page 103, MPM • Page 105, Milwaukee Public Library • Page 106, SHSW (X22)4482 • Page 107, HHBS • Page 108, left—MPM; right—OPM • Page 109, OPM • Page 110, upper—SHSW (X3)18574; lower—MPM • Page 111, MPM • Page 112, MPM • Page 113, SHSW (X3)21195 • Page 114, MPM • Page 115, OPM • Page 116, SHSW (X3)25620 • Page 117, left—MPM; right—SHSW (X3)46799 • Page 118, SHSW (X3)25621; Page 119, HHBS • Page 120, left—SHSW (X3)25617; right—SHSW (X3)20978 • Page 121, MPM • Page 122, OPM • Page 123, SHSW (X3)17183 • Page 124, HHBS • Page 125, MPM • Page 126, MCHS • Page 126-127, Milwaukee Public Library • Page 127, OPM • Page 128, MCHS • Page 129, MPM • Page 131, OPM • Page 132, Circus World Museum • Page 133, Circus World Museum • Page 134, Circus World Museum • Page 134-135, Circus World Museum • Page 135, HHBS • Page 136, SHSW (B5)281 • Page 137, OPM • Page 138, OPM • Page 138-139, OPM • Page 139, OPM • Page 140, SHSW (V24)2009 • Page 141, SHSW (W6)24981 • Page 142, HHBS • Page 143, SHSW (B531)332 • Page 144, HHBS • Page 145, upper—SHSW (S86)76; lower—HHBS • Page 146, upper—Carl Bernard; lower—MPM • Page 147, MPM • Page 148, SHSW (X3)25588 • Page 149, upper—SHSW (X3)19749; lower—SHSW (T355)68 • Page 150, HHBS • Page 151, HHBS • Page 153, SHSW (V24/D)2003 • Page 154, HHBS • Page 155, left—SHSW (V24/D)2001; right—Virginia Williams • Page 156, SHSW (X3)25623 • Page 157, upper—SHSW (V24/D)2045; lower—SHSW (V24/D)2043 • Page 158, OPM • Page 159, upper—SHSW; lower—OPM • Page 160, SHSW (X3)21264 • Page 161, SHSW (X3)25589 • Page 162, MCHS • Page 162-163, MCHS • Page 163, SHSW (X28)3723 • Page 164, left—OPM; right—Mrs. Arthur Weber • Page 165, SHSW (X3)25591 • Page 166, lower—Mr. and Mrs. Jame Stone; upper—OPM • Page 166-167, OPM • Page 168, SHSW (X32)5235 • Page 169, SHSW (X3)14090 • Page 170, SHSW (X3)2696 • Page 171, SHSW (X3)11092 • Page 172, left—MPM; right—Mr. and Mrs. Edward Mahnke • Page 173, OPM • Page 174-175, SHSW (V2/D)722 • Page 175, HHBS.

Caption Credits

Page 6 Curtis, John T., *The Vegetation of Wisconsin* (Madison, 1959).

Page 22 Draper, Lyman and Croffut, William, *A Helping Hand for Town and Country: An American Home Book of Practical and Scientific Information* (1870). Freeman, Samuel, *The Emigrant's Hand Book and Guide to Wisconsin* (1851).

Page 25 Freeman, op. cit.

Page 30 Draper and Croffut, op. cit.

Page 34 Draper and Croffut, op. cit.

Page 36 Holmes, Fred L., *Side Roads: Excursions into Wisconsin's Past* (Madison, 1949).

Page 45 Draper and Croffut, op. cit.

Page 50 McGinnis, R. J., *The Good Old Days* (New York, 1960). Kraus, Michael and Vera, *Family Album for Americans* (New York, 1961).

Page 53 Austin, H. Russell, *The Wisconsin Story* (Milwaukee, 1948).

Page 55 Baumann, Edward W., "Hall of Flame," *Exclusively Yours*, May 5, 1969.

Page 62 Holmes, op. cit.

Page 68 Kraus, op. cit.

Page 70 McGinnis, op. cit.

Page 76 *The Story of the Green Bay and Western*, Bulletin 115, Railway and Locomotive Historical Society (Boston, 1966). Cohn, David L., *The Good Old Days* (New York, 1940).

Page 104 Chapman, Silas, *Hand Book of Wisconsin* (Milwaukee, 1855).

Page 115 Holmes, op. cit.

Page 127 Holmes, op. cit.

Page 130 Dulles, Foster Rhea, *America Learns to Play* (New York, 1940).

Page 148 Draper and Croffut, op. cit.

Page 152 Freeman, op. cit.

Page 153 Radin, Paul, *The Winnebago Tribe* (Washington, 1923).

Page 158 Shannon, Fred A., *The Farmer's Last Frontier* (New York, 1945).

Page 160 Muir, John, *The Story of My Boyhood and Youth* (New York, 1912).